THE EXTREMELY SERIOUS GUIDE TO SEX

'What a daft title for a painting . . . "Page Three"!'

THE EXTREMELY SERIOUS GUIDE TO

SEX

KEITH RAY

COLUMBUS BOOKS
LONDON

'Sex is like an aubergine . . . I just can't for the life of me remember why . . . '

Anon.

Other books in the *Extremely Serious* series:
The Extremely Serious Guide to Fitness and Health
The Extremely Serious Guide to Class
The Extremely Serious Guide to Business
The Extremely Serious Guide to Parenthood
The Extremely Serious Guide to Moving House
The Extremely Serious Guide to Sin
The Extremely Serious Guide to Gardening

First published in Great Britain in 1985 by
Columbus Books Limited
19-23 Ludgate Hill, London EC4M 7PD

Reprinted 1985, 1987, 1988

Designed by Rupert Kirby

Typeset by Falcon Graphic Art Ltd
Wallington, Surrey
Printed and bound by Richard Clay Limited
Bungay, Suffolk

ISBN 0 86287 240 5

CONTENTS

ACKNOWLEDGEMENTS

In the preparation of this book the author is especially indebted to Miss ***** of Swansea, Dr and Mrs ********** of Beaconsfield, Miss ** and Miss ** ******* of Edinburgh, the Very Reverend ****, Canon and Mrs ******, Sister ***** and the Nuns of the Convent of St ******, His Serene Highness the ****** of ************, Mr Justice ********, and the ***** Ladies' College 2nd Lacrosse Team.

PREFACE

Sex is the most popular sport in the world. It has been estimated that around 98 per cent of the population are, at some time in their lives, sexually active. This makes sex five times as popular as jogging, 15 times as popular as tennis or squash, 25 times as popular as swimming or golf, and about 698 times as popular as hang-gliding. And yet the shelves of our bookshops are woefully deficient in general handbooks on the subject. Certainly there are books on various exciting and often impossible positions, and books on way-out sexual problems, but there are few if any all-embracing user-guides to sex. This is where this book is intended to fit in. If you are sexually active, or can at least remember the day when you were, then this book is for you.

'Hey, Mum, why does Uncle Harry only come round after Daddy's gone to work?'

INTRODUCTION

The reader, picking this book up for the first time, might quite legitimately question the need for yet another book about sex. 'Surely,' I can hear him say, 'we are already swamped with books about sex . . . and in any case what good do books do . . . you can only learn about sex by DOING it!' Now, whilst I wholeheartedly support the concept of learning about sex 'on-the-job', as it were, I maintain that this little book fills a real and as yet unbridged gap in the available literature on the subject. To illustrate why I believe this to be so we must look back at how this book came to be written.

It all started one warm September afternoon a couple of years ago. A very good friend of mine (whom for the sake of anonymity we shall call Fred) and his wife were indulging in a frantic, pleasantly naughty, session of totally unbridled passion on their sitting-room carpet. (I hasten to add, for the benefit of the more prudish readers, and those of a prurient nature, that the curtains were drawn, the telephone was off the hook, and the children were safely occupied for the day at school; and the lady concerned really was his lawfully wedded wife of many years' standing.)

Half-time arrived, and I, or rather I mean my good friend Fred, emerged for a breather feeling stiff, tired, hungry and very, very hot. Fred desperately needed four things: some loosening-up exercises; a simple way of improving his stamina; some good gonad-nourishing food, and a way of cooling down his over-exerted body. Not a particularly tall order, I can hear you saying. Seeking inspiration and advice Fred groped his way towards his bookcase naïvely believing that his extensive collection of literature on the subject would provide the speedy answer. He was wrong. Although there were books on psycho-sexual problems, and books of sexual positions and techniques, and books on dieting and sex, there was no single all-round compendium on the subject which would answer all his questions. A subsequent two-hour search of the shelves in the public library (he was fully dressed at this point) proved equally fruitless, and to top it all when he got home his wife had got fed up waiting and had returned to doing the ironing. From a sexual point of view the afternoon had been a write-off.

This was the sorry tale that my very good friend Fred related over a pint in the local that September evening. It made me decide that, if no all-embracing sexual reference manual existed, then it was my duty to write one to save adult society, and Fred in particular, from wasted afternoons. That evening when the children had finally gone to bed, and the house was in peace again, my wife and I sat down together to discuss and draw up a specification for this exciting new literary adventure. It didn't take long to define the task that faced us:

- the book should be, and be seen to be, a highly authoritative work. My being a doctor was likely to help considerably in achieving this objective. The fact that I was a doctor of engineering, rather than medicine, I saw as a minor inconvenience rather than a real problem.
- it should be an extremely serious book of sex, because sex is indeed an extremely serious subject. With typical inspirational genius this led my wife to suggest the eventual title of the book.
- it should be an inexpensive book in order to leave the reader plenty of cash to actually enjoy him/herself. (Although sex itself is normally free, it is my experience that the trappings of sex, which go to create the ever so vital atmosphere, are wickedly expensive.)
- the book should be heatproof, sweatproof and stain-resistant in order to withstand the rigours of even the most passionately occupied bed.
- it should be published in a small format so that it may be discreetly slipped under pillows or inside pants and knickers. At the same time it should not be so thick a volume as to present risk of physical injury when so concealed.
- the print should be sufficiently large that it may be comfortably read from a distance of 4′ 6″ by the average adult without glasses. (This distance was carefully calculated to be the maximum distance between the eye and the hand in the most adventurous but legal sexual position in common use today. It subsequently became necessary to increase this to 4′ 9″ when the book became available in Scandinavia.)
- it should be a paperback of approximately 100 pages. My own extensive research has shown that this is the optimum size of book for holding steady at the critical moment of orgasm.
- it should be available on prescription.

In retrospect we feel we succeeded in most of our objectives. The only serious shortfall is that the book is still not available on prescription, but we live in hope that the Department of Health and Social Security will eventually come to its senses. We earnestly feel that this book fulfils just as important a role in the medical repertoire as any paracetamol tablet or antibiotic, but progress in medical science is often notoriously slow. For the second edition we are planning two minor modifications.

Firstly, we plan to make the entire book edible; this will not only provide useful emergency sustenance to the reader, but should assist in speedy disposal of the volume when caught *in flagrante delicto*. Secondly, we propose to make every fourth page a contraceptive film; although technically quite simple, we have encountered religious opposition to this proposal, and according to the printer it is quite difficult to get the ink to take.

The final manuscript was the result of many, many hours of hard research by the author. Indeed the research was so hard and exhausting that he has all but given up sex, channelling what little bit of energy he has left into collecting the more timid varieties of butterfly.

To be on the safe side, keep this book under the pillow at all times.

WHAT IS SEX?

(This section has been left blank intentionally. If the reader feels there is any need for a section with this title then he, or she, is not really ready for this volume. Perhaps the reader should consider instead something more introductory such as *Janet and John Discover They Are Different*; *Sex at Pooh Corner; Wind and Other Things in the Willows; Paddington Bare* or *Biggles' Flies Undone*. Then, when he, or she, realizes this section is unnecessary he, or she, can go straight on to the next part of the book without fear or trepidation.)

'You'll have to cut down on sex, Mr Jones. After all, you're only 25.'

ARE YOU FIT ENOUGH FOR SEX?

Sex is a very demanding activity, and just as no one would dream of competing in an Olympic marathon if they were not fit, so no one should consider indulging in sexual activity unless they are physically up to it. From the point of view of sex there are four vitally important elements of fitness:

- stamina (to help keep things going)
- co-ordination (to make sure they go in the right places)
- agility (to make sure you can get them to these places)
- memory (to make sure you can remember what they are going there for)

The following simple tests should help the reader to decide whether they really are up to sex, or whether perhaps they should take up butterfly collecting or watching television instead. Complete the series of four tests and score yourself honestly. Add up your total score and then look up your sexual fitness rating in the table at the end of this section.

A Test for Stamina

In order to keep going during long sessions of sexual activity (especially in organized groups of twenty or more) it is essential that you possess a high degree of stamina. A good test of stamina is the common or garden press-up. For this test you will need a clear area of soft carpet (avoid the more erotic colours and textures which might merely distract you from the serious matter in hand) and a stop-watch. Lie on the floor face-down, set the stop-watch to run one minute, and then see how many press-ups you can complete before the time runs out. Score your performance as follows:

- if you managed a scorching 3000 press-ups or more in the first 30 seconds, half of these being accomplished without using your arms but just by exhaling smartly, and then quietly sloped off to refute the theory of relativity over 25 pints of bitter score 100
- if you managed at least 1500 press-ups, left the carpet smoking but failed to refute Einstein's masterpiece score 85
- if you managed only 250 press-ups and detected a significantly raised pulse at the end score 70
- if you managed only 10 press-ups and were out of breath at the end score 15
- if you managed the press-up OK but had to get help from a friend for the pressdown score 10
- if you managed to lie on the floor unassisted but needed two weeks' bed-rest in the Bahamas before carrying on score 6
- if you are still struggling to set the stop-watch score 2
- if you were unable even to read the instructions without first slackening your belt, removing your watch, false teeth and glasses, and going on a high-fibre, low-carbohydrate diet for a week score 1

Note:
If the press-ups induced an orgasm, but you still managed 20 or more, add 5 points to your score.

If your stomach is so large that when you lie on your front your arms just flail helplessly in mid-air remove 10 points.

If you find you prefer press-ups to sex, stop reading this book at once and join your local gym.

If at the end of the test you could not return your arms to your sides remove 5 points, and if you did not even want to deduct 2 more.

If you managed to sneak off part way through the test for sex but still managed to return and complete more than 40 press-ups within the minute, double your score.

A Test for Co-ordination

During sex a high degree of co-ordination is required to ensure that the right things get put in the right places at the right time; poor co-ordination can result in severe impact injuries and extreme disappointment. The following test should help the reader to decide whether special care is required in this area. Stand upright, and place your right hand, palm down, on top of your head. Stretch your left arm out in front of you with the index finger pointing outwards. Then start to describe circles on the top of your head with your right palm while simultaneously touching in turn with your left index finger firstly your left ear lobe, then your nose, and then your right ear lobe. Keep up this movement for as long as possible, and time how long elapses before you break the rhythm. Score your performance as follows:

- if you encountered no difficulty at all but got rather bored after the first two months and switched to using your feet instead score 100
- if you managed to keep going until your scalp glowed and your ear lobes suffered severe compaction score 82
- if you managed a full minute before going wrong score 60
- if you managed the circles with your right hand but got your left finger stuck in your ear score 52
- if you only managed to get your right hand up to ear level before passing out from exhaustion score 20
- if you toppled over while adopting the starting position score 16
- if you toppled over but did not realize score 6
- if you are still trying to look up the word co-ordination in your dictionary score 5
- if you are still trying, for the 28th time, to pick the dictionary up off the floor where you dropped it score 3
- if you are still trying to remember which is right and which is left score 1

Note:
If at the end of this test you decide you rather like having a finger stuck in your ear deduct 10 points.

If deducting the points induces an orgasm deduct 5 more and have another.

If you had to get a friend to do the rubbing and touching for you subtract 12 points. If you rather enjoyed this and started phoning round your friends to organize a rubbing and touching party deduct 5 more, but have fun.

If you cannot pronounce the word 'co-ordination' in a standing position without first lowering your trousers and taking a cold shower skip the rest of this chapter.

'Speaking as an old rugby player, I've scored twelve points . . . four unconverted tries.'

A Test for Agility

Agility is all about being able to assume different positions with accuracy and speed, and with the minimum of lasting physical injury. For all but the most mundane and boring forms of sexual activity a high degree of agility is a fundamental requirement. It is also important that both partners (or all of those involved if there are more than two) are equally agile otherwise there is a real risk of misunderstanding. The following test should allow the reader to decide whether he or she is currently agile enough, or whether remedial action is called for.

The object of this test is to assess whether you are agile enough to place your right leg behind your neck without experiencing severe pain or loss of memory. Simply sit on the floor, and grasping your right foot with both hands carefully, and slowly, pull the foot towards you until you can comfortably place your leg behind your neck. Score your performance in the following way:

- if you managed to get your leg round your neck twice or more and return the foot to the floor on the other side score 100
- if you managed to get the leg behind your head without discomfort and managed to hold this position for a full week without losing your job or your memory score 82
- if you just managed it with the assistance of two helpers (if they were scantily clad nymphets stop the test at once) score 70
- if you could only get your foot to face level score 62
- if you could only just get your foot clear of the ground score 51
- if you couldn't reach your foot at all score 30
- if you couldn't even see your foot because of your stomach score 12
- if you couldn't even remember where your foot is, or what it looks like, and tried to grasp some other, nearer, part of your body instead score 8
- if you found a bit of your body which you liked pulling score 6
- if you are still trying to sit down score 4
- if you are still trying to straighten up after the stamina test score 1

Note:
If your final score is less than your shoe size deduct five points.

If your score is less than your shoe size but you did manage to place your leg in the right position you should see a chiropodist without delay.

If you find you prefer life with your right leg behind your head, and your career improves as a result, deduct 6 points from your score for each promotion obtained within the first four weeks.

If after the test your social life improves add 5 points and if the result is even, double it and take the square root; if the answer is less than 4.5 add ten, double it and deduct 6. If you get the sum wrong double it again. If you still get the sum wrong, forget it and score 20 instead.

A Test for Memory

A good memory is a vital prerequisite for good sex. It is important that both partners remember what sex is, how you do it, what goes where, why, and for how long. And above all it is vital that you remember whether or not you have done it before with the partner concerned, and what the partner's name is. (Few things are better guaranteed to ruin sex than calling your partner by the wrong name, especially if it is a name for the wrong sex.) If you suspect that you might have a problem in this area then it might be best to stick to partners with the same name, and perhaps to go for unisex names like Leslie/Lesley or Francis/Frances, etc. You may test your memory power by answering the following questions honestly:

- you can remember most things from five years ago score 100
- if you can remember many things from five years ago score 90
- if you can remember at least two things score 80
- if you can remember two things, but cannot remember if they are actually different things score 50
- if you cannot remember anything from five years ago score 38
- if you cannot even remember how to count up to five without using your fingers score 20
- if you cannot remember where you left your fingers score 15
- if you have forgotten what the test was all about score 11
- if you have forgotten whether you ever paid for this book send £3.95 direct to the author and score 8
- if you have forgotten how to read you won't be able to read this anyway, but you would have scored 4
- if you have forgotten how to read but didn't even notice and carried on regardless score 1

'Look, Mabel – it's the chambermaid from our hotel.'

At the end of these tests you should add up your total score. If you are still lying on the floor with your leg behind your neck with one finger stuck up a nostril doing a press-up whilst trying to remember what the digit five looks like forget this addition and assume your total score is 20. Interpret your total score as follows:

score 400+	You lied about your score, but you should not really have any great problems with sex if you can find a partner willing to tolerate a cocky little shit like yourself.
score 300–400	You are ready for anything involving groups of up to 20 active participants and lasting for up to 20 hours between meal breaks, including generous helpings of flagellation, bondage and schoolgirl uniforms.
score 200–300	You are ready for most things, but it might be wise to limit yourself to the one bond or two, and to limit the group to 3 or 4. Suggest meal breaks every two hours.
score 100–200	You are fit for most normal sex in doses lasting up to one hour, but it might be best to stick to the same partner so that not too much time and energy is spent establishing partner's name, sex, etc.
score 50–100	It might be best to stick to voyeurism or the occasional heavy breathing session on the telephone.
score 20–50	It might be best to stick to dirty magazines.
score 10–20	Make it the *Reader's Digest*. Not only will you find it less demanding than sex, but you might also enjoy it more.
score 0–5	Stop reading this book at once. It might prove to be fatally erotic.

Note:
If you were too busy having sex to undertake this test you do not have any serious problem.

If you never reach this page you might have a problem but you will never find out.

If you found adding up the score more taxing than the tests you will probably have no problem with sex but should not nourish any ambition to become a chartered accountant.

If adding up the score resulted in an earth-shattering orgasm then you might well be trainable as a statistician but should avoid it on health grounds.

If you are still trying to get down on the floor for your first press-up then you should consider a life of celibacy.

'Nobody's perfect.'

'You're just not good enough for me.'

'The doctor says I need more exercise, so could you struggle a bit tonight?'

ENERGY REQUIREMENTS OF SEX

Sex is a very physically demanding activity which requires in its most advanced forms considerable amounts of energy. It is wise for the sexually active adult to be aware of these energy needs and to plan an eating schedule accordingly. Nothing can be worse than one or both partners passing out from hypoglycaemia part way through. A full list of energy requirements for all variations of sexual activity is outside the range of this book, but the following examples will give the reader some rough idea of the range of requirements which may have to be met in practice:

Getting undressed using both hands	25 calories
Getting undressed using one hand	80 calories
Getting undressed using teeth	120 calories
Getting undressed by sucking hard	1050 calories
Getting into bed using both legs	10 calories
Getting into bed using one leg	22 calories
Getting into bed on all fours	50 calories
Getting into bed using trampoline (high ceiling)	8 calories
Getting into bed using trampoline (low ceiling)	180 calories
Warming the bed up by writhing (alone)	75 calories
Warming the bed up by writhing (with partner)	50 calories
Foreplay: whipping (per whip)	5 calories
bondage (per bond)	15 calories
stroking (per stroke)	8 calories
bondage with spaghetti (per strand) (add 15 calories if you also eat it)	12 calories
Intercourse: missionary (per minute)	50 calories
non-missionary (per minute)	1900–1200 calories
illegal (per minute)	9000–2500 calories
Orgasm: ordinary single	80 calories
multiple (for each of the first ten)	79 calories
multiple (all subsequent)	179 calories
Finding the bathroom afterwards	550 calories
Showering	250 calories
Sorting out the two piles of clothes	80 calories
Getting dressed having got right pile	90 calories
Getting dressed having got wrong pile	900 calories

THE IDEAL PARTNER

'Share a room on your honeymoon?
I always suspected you were a pennypincher.'

It is impossible to draw a picture of the ideal partner, as tastes vary so much from individual to individual. However, there are some basic requirements which should be seen as an absolute minimum, on top of which personal preferences may be added. These are as follows:

'We're just not suited.'

The Male Partner

- he should be clean, neat, tidy and well-groomed, especially from the waist down.
- he should never fall down on the job.
- he should always last the distance.
- he should never smell of beer and/or Stilton cheese.
- he should not keep asking 'How are you doing?' during sex.
- he should always remove his shoes and overcoat in bed (unless of course these happen to turn you on, in which case he should be naturally aware of it).
- he shouldn't keep one eye on the TV waiting for the soccer match to start.
- he should have a sense of humour (but conversely should not laugh when you are enjoying an explosive orgasm).
- he should be fluent in at least four different positions, and have a working knowledge of at least 6 others.
- he should have his own hair and teeth.
- he shouldn't compare you with his mother.
- he shouldn't compare you with his wife.
- he shouldn't compare you with his dog, cat or budgie.
- he should be able to see his toes from a standing position without having to use a mirror.

The Female Partners

- she should always manage to stay awake throughout.
- she should never ask what's on TV halfway through.
- her moaning should neither be so quiet that you need a stethoscope to tell whether she is enjoying it, nor so loud that the neighbours are disturbed.
- she shouldn't smell of beer and/or Stilton cheese.
- she should be capable of having and enjoying multiple orgasms even under adverse conditions (such as a tax appeal, when the tax commissioner happens to be your mother).
- she should be able to reach the first orgasm within 15 seconds, and to produce one each minute subsequently on the minute.
- she shouldn't keep asking 'How much longer are you going to be?'
- she should never say 'Was that it?'
- she should never say 'What was that?'
- she shouldn't giggle when you undress.
- she shouldn't study for an Open University degree during foreplay.
- she should have her own teeth, hair and breasts.
- she should enjoy getting a bit frisky.
- she should be able to stand upright without her breasts dragging on the carpet.
- she should not be looking for a father figure.
- she should not be looking for a mother figure.
- she should not be looking for a hamster substitute.

THE INITIAL INTRODUCTION

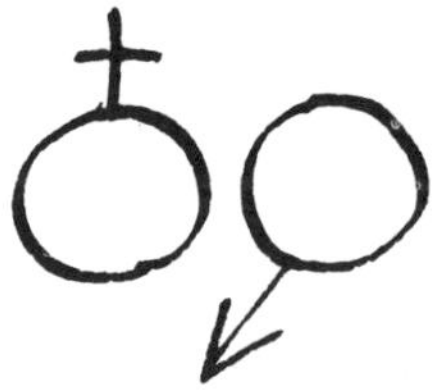

'So you're Australian, too.'

The impression left by the first few words exchanged between a man and a woman can fundamentally influence the subsequent development of the relationship. In other words, get those first few words wrong and the relationship will be a non-starter; but get them right and romance can blossom. There are no rigid rights and wrongs about the initial introduction, but the following guidelines might prove useful.

THINGS TO AVOID SAYING:

You are under arrest. This is not a good way to begin a lasting relationship as bail cannot be guaranteed.

How much do you charge? This will instantly alienate most prospective partners. But be especially aware of anyone who instantly responds with a quote, particularly if it is on the low side.

I recognize the smell but cannot remember your name. Avoid this opening, even if it happens to be true.

You remind me of my mother/father. This can be especially damaging if, for instance, the comparison is drawn with the parent of the opposite sex. Few women enjoy being likened to a man's father.

You remind me of my grandmother/ grandfather.

You remind me of my dog. Strangely, in the case of the British, this is often taken as less of an insult than the previous two examples.

I didn't realize it was a fancy dress party (when it wasn't).

How about it? This is really a bit too blunt for most people at the first encounter, especially if said by the woman.

Do you come here often? In a real emergency this is acceptable, as it rarely causes actual offence. If you are going to start off with a question you might as well make it a useful one, such as 'what time is it?' or 'what's your name?', or 'will you lend me a quid?'

Do you come often? Sometimes this abbreviated form of the previous question is used inadvertently. Again beware of partners who, as the very first thing they say to you, reply with a confident 'yes' or 'no'.

Do you often? A further abbreviated form. Avoid.

Do you? Similarly be on your guard if this question produces an unsurprised and instantaneous response in the affirmative.

Are you real/serious/authentic, etc.?

You make my loins blush. This is certainly a bit blunt for the first encounter. Save it for the second date.

'I never forget a face, Miss Williams.'

TRY INSTEAD:

I've seen you on television, haven't I?

Aren't you one of the Pirelli girls? Women should avoid saying this to a man.

You inspire a chap to question the fundamental validity of the whole concept of relativity. This may sound a bit heavy, but it is likely to impress. If the conversation develops into a discussion of the general theory, forget it!

You light up my soul and give meaning to life.

You are truly one of God's masterpieces.

The Mona Lisa can't hold a candle to you. This has the added virtue of being technically correct.

You redefined the upper limit on my scale of beauty.

You remind me of a dewy morning.

LOVE LETTERS

'Dear Mr Jones, further to your fabulous knees of the 15th . . .'

One of the essential ingredients of the more romantic types of sexual involvement is the love letter. Love letters play a key role in keeping any relationship intact, especially when periods of separation are involved. The content of such a letter is clearly of paramount importance, and whilst the precise choice of words must always remain an individual decision there are certain golden rules and general guidelines which are worth mentioning here.

- avoid too much factual content. Do not, for example, say things like 'I trimmed my toenails yesterday', or 'The grass grew 2.5mm last week, and precipitation totalled 1.39cm'. The ideal love letter should actually say virtually nothing whilst sacrificing little in length.
- avoid excessive formality (such as 'Dear Sir' or 'Dear Madam', and 'Yours faithfully') as well as excessive familiarity (such as 'Hi, cock' or 'wotcha, you old turd').
- never start the letter with 'To whom it may concern'. Always use your beloved's name, and be sure to get his or her name correct. And above all get the sex right.
- adopt a free-flowing, easy style. Avoid clumsy styles like 'Further to my love letter of the 2nd inst' or 'I beg to inform you that', and never finish off with 'I remain, Madam, your obedient lover . . . '
- always write the letter yourself. A letter signed 'Mrs H. Jones, pp your loving sweetheart' carries much less weight in the game of love.
- pay special attention to spelling. Referring to your beloved as your sweetheart sounds much better than referring to him or her as, for example, your sweatheart.
- write the letter by hand. A typed letter is nothing like as romantic. And in particular avoid xerox copies and carbons.
- always put the correct postage on the letter. Although it is likely in practice that the recipient would pay the excess postal charge (and indeed unstamped letters often reach their destination more quickly than their stamped counterparts) there is always the risk that if the stamp is omitted regularly your beloved may develop a more meaningful relationship with the postman.
- the best paper to use is a soft pastel shade. Failing this pure white is acceptable. Avoid the false economy of using the reverse side of old business letters or bills.
- avoid manilla 'window' envelopes, and envelopes with 'Final Demand' printed on the outside.
- feel free to use flowery romantic speech (dew, daffodils, clouds, misty mornings, etc. are all fine) but avoid technical terms (condensed atmospheric vapour in ground-borne droplet form, yellow flowers of the genus narcissus, cumulo nimbus, pre-noon temporal situations exhibiting super-saturation moisture condition symptoms, etc. are less romantic).
- never address your love letter to 'Miss J. Richards or Occupier'; this suggests a serious lack of commitment.
- avoid excessive length (after the first 250 pages even the most romantic love letter begins to pall) and excessive brevity.

'I love you.'

CREATING A MOOD

Before any really satisfying sexual activity can take place, it is necessary to create a romantic mood. This is rather like painting a picture or writing an overture; care must be taken at each stage to build on the progress so far achieved, and add to the total mood until it all comes together in a romantic masterpiece of mutual sexuality (or at least until you both feel randy). Some of the components which may go into creating the mood are as follows:

Soft lighting The lighting should be dark, and the colour soft. Bright green spotlights or numerous fluorescent strips are not designed with romance in mind. On the other hand don't let the lighting get too dark otherwise you may have difficulty actually locating your partner.

Music The best music is slow, soft and light. Many light classical pieces are fine, as are Semprini and others of his type. Avoid brass bands, Stockhausen, Mahler, synthetic electronic music, and the more lively types of rock and country and western. Also avoid the false economy of singing yourself even if your voice is good; when things start warming up you may find it difficult to continue the musical accompaniment unaided.

Dancing It can be very romantic to take your partner gently in your arms and quietly waltz around the room in the candlelight. Stick to the waltz or some other slow dance performed in close formation. Avoid rock-and-roll, the tango and the highland fling.

Reading With some partners reading a mildly titillating novel or glancing through an erotic magazine can work wonders. But avoid the Bible, the telephone directory, medical textbooks and car maintenance manuals.

Drink Alcohol, in moderation, can act as a good aphrodisiac. Champagne or a gently sparkling rosé are best; avoid rough gin straight from the bottle, your home-made parsnip and radish, and steer clear of beer if you want to create a good impression. Avoid at all costs false economies such as meths or white spirit, unless you just want to get someone drunk to have a quick bang.

Talking Just talking to your partner can be a very effective mood creator, provided you stick to the right topics. Keep to compliments about your partner's beauty, or how your heart is in a constant state of turmoil since you met, or how love makes every season seem like spring; avoid discussions about energy prices, the blocked drain you discovered earlier, the balance of payments crisis, earth-moving equipment, AIDS and other sexually related complaints, and arguments about the ideal shape for a toothbrush.

Clothes Dressing correctly can help the mood a lot. Men should stick to casual, loose clothing; a smart pair of jeans and a silk shirt with the top three buttons undone is usually fine. Anoraks, boiler suits, scuba-diving gear, armour, deer-stalkers, crash helmets and policeman's uniform are not recommended. Women are advised to wear a romantic loose-flowing or figure-hugging, dress in black or some simple pastel shade; giant fluorescent flower patterns, old baggy men's trousers, dungarees, maternity dresses, inflatable slim-suits, and anything made of rubber are not a good idea.

HOW TO BRING UP THE SUBJECT OF SEX

Suppose you have got to know your partner reasonably well, and you now decide the time has arrived for your relationship to become a bit more intimate. How should you raise the sensitive question of sex? There are many ways in which this can be done, some being a lot better in most circumstances than others. Below we give examples of some of the more common approaches to this problem:

- serve that intimate dinner for two in the bedroom. Some partners may feel that you are taking one or two things for granted, but if it does work then at least you will not have to walk far on a full stomach.
- just say 'How about it, then?' This is becoming more acceptable in our permissive age, and is said nearly as often by the female as by the male. But it is really rather blunt and direct if you ever hope romance and love will creep into the relationship.
- begin an intellectual discussion about whether celibacy suppresses the auto-immune response to the influenza virus. Avoid this topic with partners who are medically qualified, or else the conversation could be unnecessarily prolonged.
- start undressing, and hope your partner follows suit.
- leave sex manuals lying around. The danger here is that your partner may fail to realize that this was done for his/her benefit, and may presume falsely that you are always in an advanced state of sexual preparation.
- show the real or simulated symptoms of a first-rate erection, and hope she notices (this is strictly for male readers: if any female reader can achieve a first-rate erection then she is probably reading the wrong book).
- show a dirty film. Helps to get you both in the mood, but check he/she is not short-sighted and not wearing glasses or lenses in order to look better; otherwise you might as well show *The Sound of Music*.
- say things like 'Your body drives my mind to the very edge of a precipice of sexual desire from which there is only one release!' Pray that he/she doesn't respond by telling you to throw yourself off it.
- put your partner over your shoulder and carry him/her off to bed. Many people like this sort of positive approach, although some men feel threatened if so carried by women of small stature.

'Don't think I haven't been tempted to play around on the side.'

SEX: WHEN TO DO IT

There are many different occasions when the sexual act may be undertaken. The best times for sex are, in the author's experience, those times when it is least expected (for example, while cleaning your teeth). It is difficult to lay down strict rules about times, and to say for instance that sex between 10.15 am and 10.17 am is 75 per cent more enjoyable than it is between 8.56 pm and 8.58 pm, partly because people's preferences vary so much and partly because two minutes is scarcely long enough for even the fastest worker to make love. There are however some very general guidelines:

BAD TIMES FOR SEX

During an auction at Sotheby's You may end up accidentally bidding for something.

During a free-fall parachute jump In itself this can be quite a good occasion as the apparent weightlessness may permit fairly adventurous positions; but there is always the risk that at the moment of orgasm you may forget to pull the ripcord.

During the marriage ceremony This suggests a lack of sensitivity, especially if your partner is not your prospective spouse.

During a row Sex is best before rows or when making up afterwards. Sex actually during a row again suggests lack of feeling.

While donating blood There is a risk of the canula being pulled out.

During open-heart surgery In the case of the patient active sex is virtually impossible, while for the surgeon it is extremely risky and suggests lack of dedication to the task in hand.

While negotiating for a new mortgage with the building society manager He will not be impressed (unless he is the partner) and you may find it hard to answer detailed questions about your current financial situation.

While voting in a General Election This is possibly illegal, being contrary to the Representation of the People Act.

GOOD TIMES FOR SEX

In the morning It tends to be more spontaneous and hence more enjoyable than at night.

During your lunch-break Even more exciting than in the morning and definitely more challenging.

During a cross-channel swim The change of rhythm is well known to help prevent cramp.

During Lent There are many better things to give up during Lent than sex.

During Ravel's *Bolero*.

During an episode of *Dallas*. Almost anything is better than actually watching the TV screen at such times.

While playing badminton Excellent training for racket control, and good for the reflexes, especially during a long rally.

When his wife/her husband is away

While competing in the Winter Olympics bobsleigh event

During the last night of the Proms Excellent for music lovers but not so good for exhibitionists as it is likely no one will even notice.

'Where have you been?'

'This way I can tell my wife quite honestly that I haven't set eyes on another woman.'

SEX: WHERE TO DO IT

There is an almost infinite variety of places suitable for indulging in sexual activity, ranging from the purely mundane (e.g. bed) through the more exciting and romantic (e.g. on the dewy grass under a full moon) to the positively adventurous (e.g. inside a tumble drier). Couples who stick rigidly to one location are likely in time to find the excitement in their relationship waning; this is technically known as the environmentally induced sexual enjoyment reduction syndrome (or, as the sexual psychologists call it, boredom). To help sexually bored people rekindle the flame of excitement we suggest here some alternative locations where they might experiment:

The back seat of a Mini This is an old favourite, but its popularity and effectiveness never wanes. The very challenge of getting it together in this cramped location is one of the most effective aphrodisiacs known to man.

On the roofrack of a Mini This has all the excitement of the Mini's rear seat, but with added naughtiness and the risk of being seen, especially if the vehicle concerned is travelling up the M1 on a Friday evening.

Underneath a Mini Interesting, but for slim people only. It's best to be a member of the AA in case anything should go wrong.

Inside a telephone kiosk (standing up).

Inside a telephone kiosk (lying down).

On the beach Always a favourite, and avoiding the particles of sand makes such occasions especially memorable.

In a hammock This can be real fun, especially in high wind out of doors. It is best to try to make love in time with the natural frequency of the hammock's swing, otherwise extraordinary amounts of energy may be consumed.

On a Boeing 747 Always the favourite aeroplane for sex as it has so many quiet corners. The best locations are one of the rear window seats or the kitchen area. The flight deck is, unfortunately, only available to the crew, but provides the best location of all, particularly during take-off and landing.

On a roller-coaster This is good for the more gregarious lovers. May be a bit too congested for many positions on Bank Holidays.

Trafalgar Square A good place for sex if you want to be noticed (for example, if your lover is someone really famous).

In the dock at the Old Bailey One of the naughtiest places for sex, especially when the verdict is being returned.

In the witness box of the Old Bailey Very challenging, especially if you are being cross-examined at the time and the defence counsel is your partner.

In the bath (jacuzzi especially). Again an old favourite, but a really excellent location.

The hard shoulder of the M4 Very exciting if the traffic is heavy, but there is a health risk associated with the exhaust fumes. Also watch out for the traffic cops.

Inside a harpsichord This is as good as inside a piano, but with added novelty value. It can give a totally new meaning to the chromatic scale.

THE BED

Research has shown that over 92 per cent of all sexual activity takes place in bed. Given its important role, it is clearly vital that the bed is up to the job in hand, and as a general rule the following requirements should be satisfied:

- it should be at least two feet wide. While narrower beds can be great fun for the actual act of love-making, it is vital that the bed is wide enough to permit partners to flop to their own sides afterwards (or halfway through if things are getting really active) without fear of falling out of bed. The fear of falling on to the floor is one of the commoner causes of impotence.
- it should be no more than eight feet wide. In wider beds unnecessary time may be spent merely locating your partner.
- it should be reasonably level.
- it should not be so soft that there is risk of suffocation.
- neither should it be so hard that there is risk of impact injury.
- avoid smooth nylon sheets, in order to avoid the risk of your partner shooting out like a bar of soap when you leap on top of him/her. Cotton sheets are better as they have a higher coefficient of friction.
- avoid highly starched bedclothes, with their attendant risk of accidental castration.
- avoid plain white bedclothes as they show the damp patch more clearly than coloured ones.
- the bed must be in a good structural condition. Nothing ruins the mood more than a bed collapsing a few seconds prior to orgasm.
- the love-making surface of the bed should not be too far off the ground, otherwise there is a serious risk of injury if the participants roll off on to the floor.
- it should not be too close to the ground, otherwise draughts can be a serious problem.
- water beds are risky if either partner is prone to sea-sickness.
- the bed should not be so cold as to kill passion, nor so warm that there is no incentive to warm up.
- there should be plenty of pillows available so as not to limit the feasible range of sexual positions.
- some authorities claim that a magnetic north/south orientation promotes passion. The author remains open-minded on this subject, but points out the advantage of having to test out many different magnetic orientations.

THE BEDROOM

Given that the vast majority of sexual activity takes place in bed it is important to consider what the ideal bedroom should be like. (This presupposes, of course, that the bed is in the bedroom; this need not be so, but it does tend to offer more privacy than having the bed in the kitchen or hallway, for example.) The fundamental requirements of the bedroom are that it is weatherproof, relatively immune from other distracting activities, and reasonably private. On top of these fundamental characteristics it is also desirable that the bedroom should:

- having a ceiling height greater than 3 feet 6 inches (otherwise impact injury may easily result) but less than 18 feet 9 inches (otherwise it begins to lack the degree of cosiness required for such an intimate occasion; however, if the ceiling height is very much greater than 18 feet 9 inches there is a chance that clouds may form, and this can in fact be quite romantic).
- be contained within the existing three dimensions of space, and be subject to the normal rules of gravity and the laws of motion. Love-making is not really a good time to endeavour to push back the frontiers of physics.
- have the rent/mortgage fully paid to date. The uninvited attention of a rent collector or building society manager is one of the most efficient ways of killing off any romantic mood; and if the rent collector or building society manager is your chosen partner then there is a serious risk of a permanent breakdown in the relationship.
- face east. This is so that on the following morning you may be gently woken up by the sunrise.
- have a structurally sound, but plain coloured, ceiling. Plaster falling in your partner's face, and distracting ceiling patterns, are guaranteed passion-killers.
- be simply yet tastefully furnished. If you must go in for genuine Louis XIV bedroom furniture then for heaven's sake make sure your partner is not one of those people who, at the moment of orgasm, is prone to throwing pillows, wine bottles, beds or partners around. Better to keep to simple furniture and live comfortably in the hope of finding such a spirited and carefree lover.
- not too dark. You don't want to waste precious time and energy groping around to locate your partner.
- not be too light. Avoid spotlights in the bedroom. Keep the lighting subdued; if you must use candles use one candle for each 16 square feet of bedroom area, whereas if you use electric light aim for around 30 watts maximum to be available when things start to warm up. It is a good idea to have spare illumination available for afterwards to facilitate finding the tissues, your pants, the bathroom etc.

- not be too clinical in appearance. Avoid a room which just has a bed and a box of tissues; this appears rather threatening. A few books scattered around are good, as are plants and a few discreet ornaments. Avoid leaving motorcycle gearboxes, knitting (if you are a man), half-eaten meals, dirty laundry, bits of a hand-glider, other men, or women, etc. lying around. Have a good tidy-up before things get too active.

'You could at least make some effort to look good for bed.'

GETTING UNDRESSED

In its simplest form getting undressed is nothing more than taking your clothes off. However, more sophisticated lovers recognize that how you get undressed reveals a lot about your personality, and indeed getting undressed is something of an art in its own right. Some of the more common manifestations of this art are as follows:

- all clothes removed in one long, smooth sweeping motion of the right hand. This indicates a really experienced lover.
- all clothes removed in one long, smooth sweeping motion of the left hand. This indicates a really experienced left-handed lover.
- all clothes removed in one long, smooth sweeping motion of the right foot. This indicates a quite exceptionally experienced lover who knows better things to do with his/her hands than simply undo buttons and zips.
- getting undressed behind the curtains. This suggests a shy lover, or one with something to hide.
- getting undressed inside the wardrobe. This suggests even worse shyness or something more serious to hide.
- getting undressed meticulously one garment at a time, each being carefully folded and put away in the drawer. This indicates a really particular and neat lover.
- ditto, but using feet only. This suggests a meticulous but exceedingly experienced and skilled lover.
- letting your partner undress you. This suggests a passionate nature, or maybe just a degree of laziness.
- being always undressed just in case. This suggests a lover who always lives in hope, or is exceedingly poor.
- not getting undressed at all. This suggests a lover who enjoys a challenge.
- getting undressed using teeth only. One of the most adventurous types of lover who can easily keep arms and legs fully occupied even before getting into bed.
- getting undressed merely by sucking hard. The most experienced type of lover, and something of an extrovert.

GETTING INTO BED

Getting into bed is much more than merely abandoning a vertical posture for a horizontal position on a mattress. Getting into bed is a fundamental component of the sexual act, and one in which artistic expression is permitted its full rein. How you get into bed can strongly influence what happens afterwards. Some of the more popular techniques for getting into bed are as follows:

- a sedate and slow walk from the furthest corner of the room. This usually leads to sedate and slow sex from the furthest corner of the bed.
- a frisky leap from a distance of at least 2 feet 6 inches. This suggests a certain keenness which usually precedes exciting and frisky sex.
- a leap from at least 8 feet 4 inches aided by a trampoline. This usually indicates exceptional keenness and an extraordinarily large bedroom. After such a leap you are unlikely to be disappointed.
- a crawl on all fours. This suggests either extreme exhaustion or a partner who is exceptionally drunk. In either case what follows will be scarcely worth waiting for.
- descent by greasy pole from the room above. You can be sure that the individual concerned is no novice, and has done this sort of thing before. This is one of the quickest ways of entering a bed and suggests a person of habit whose life is carefully organized and planned. It is difficult to pretend the idea of making love was purely spontaneous when your partner descends on you from above in this fashion.
- have a friend carry you into bed (the lazy man's way of getting into bed, which is unlikely to precede anything at all spectacular unless the friend can also be persuaded to join in).
- roller-skates. This is known as the Californian style, is efficient and effective and doesn't waste time unnecessarily. But make sure your partner removes the skates once in bed otherwise severe skid marks may result.
- delivery by fork-lift truck. Good for the larger partner, but the diesel fumes are a notorious passion-killer.
- by tunnelling under the quilt from the bottom end of the bed. This suggests either a very shy partner or one who starts work from the blunt end, as it were.
- some people avoid the problem of getting into bed entirely by spending their entire life in bed. This does, however, limit the scope for making new friends, and sometimes appears a bit forward, at least on the first date.

THE CONSIDERATE LOVER

Romantic, as opposed to pure lustful animal, sex is all about caring and consideration. The really considerate lover takes special care to ensure his partner's happiness and enjoyment, and whilst it is difficult to lay down strict rules about how to behave the following guidelines might be of assistance. The truly considerate lover:

- always warms his/her hands and feet.
- takes the telephone off the hook.
- stays awake throughout.
- takes his/her time about things.
- always lets you have the first orgasm.
- doesn't 'phone his/her mother half-way through.
- doesn't ask how you are doing.
- is not distracted if you fart loudly during active foreplay.
- tests the bed for broken springs beforehand and lies on that side.
- volunteers to lie on the damp patch afterwards.
- also volunteers to go and get a new box of tissues when the old one runs out, even if this involves going to the late-night drugstore.
- let's his/her partner use bathroom first.
- always removes his/her shoes, watch, pendant, etc.
- keeps going just as long as you want.
- always says it was the greatest experience since Moses came down from the mountain.
- always ensures his/her wig is secure.
- is fluent in at least six different positions.
- lets partner decide which side to flop on to afterwards.
- doesn't bring golf clubs into bed.
- doesn't invite friends to join in unless you fancy the idea.
- doesn't bring sandwiches and beer to bed.
- doesn't keep the TV on in order to ensure that the evening is not totally wasted.
- doesn't try to do the crossword at the same time even if you are rather slow.
- kisses you afterwards.

'Of course I love you as much as when we got married . . . it's just spread a little thinner nowadays.'

BRINGING THINGS TO A PREMATURE END

Sometimes it may become necessary to bring a blossoming relationship to a premature end. Sometimes this has to be done quickly; for example you may just have both ripped off your clothes and be on the point of jumping into bed when you realize he/she might just be your long-lost brother/sister. Alternatively you may discover at this point that all the things you fancied about him/her came off at the same time as the clothes, and that your partner naked is about as attractive as a packet of frozen fish fingers. Stopping the relationship instantaneously, rather than just in the morning or when you happen to have a spare moment, calls for a somewhat drastic move. Below we suggest some opening lines to introduce the idea of becoming less serious:

'I'm sorry if my crabs tickle you.'

'Before we go any further I'd like you to know, as you are someone special, that I'm AC/DC.'

'The clinic said I should be clear by now.'

'You can't change into rubber underwear, can you?'

'Do you mind if I lie on the side of the bed nearest the loo as I have this very slight problem?'

'Can I call you Mummy?'

'I hope you don't mind, but I left your phone number with my husband/wife.'

'Have you got some strong rope handy?'

'If I don't make it the address of my next-of-kin is in my wallet.'

'I don't quite know how to ask, but should I pay you now or afterwards?'

'I've only done this with sheep before, you know.'

'Just to put your mind at rest, my psychiatrist says there's no reason to worry any more . . . but don't for heaven's sake mention cucumbers!!'

Note:
In 99.99 per cent of cases any one of these openers should bring things to a speedy close. If you strike one of the 0.01 per cent of partners who get turned on by any of these statements, then you have a real problem.

FOREPLAY

Foreplay is to sex what *hors d'oeuvre* are to a good dinner. *Hors d'oeuvre* are more satisfying when you have a wide selection of dishes to choose from, and so it is with sexual foreplay. A good variety of foreplay is much better than a solid half hour spent indulging in one single titillatory activity. Many people genuinely lack imagination in this area, and as a result so much sex is boring and unsatisfying. For the sake of these readers we list below some more original forms of foreplay for them to experiment with (remember, don't stick to just one – use a good variety):

- caress your partner's tummy with a cream-covered kipper.
- watch a dirty film while smearing yourself in treacle.
- give your partner love-bites on the tongue.
- give your partner love sucks on the tongue (this is for readers whose teeth are not so good).
- try bondage using spaghetti bolognese.
- whip each other with a ripe salami.
- stroke your partner's buttocks with a bashful mole.
- tease your partner by smearing him/her in yoghurt and then lick it off, avoiding the naughty bits.
- play strip-scrabble.
- chase your partner around inside a suede-upholstered Porsche 928.
- tickle your partner with Joan Collins' head.
- stimulate your partner's lymphatic system with a battery-powered vibrator.
- have a good romp around on a water bed wearing spiked running shoes.
- open a bottle of champagne using any part of your two bodies other than hands, feet or mouth. (This is potentially dangerous.)
- feed each other dry-roasted peanuts using your thighs only.
- discover at least 25 different things to do with a Mars bar which do not involve the teeth.
- order a take-away pizza whilst both bound and gagged.
- undress each other using chopsticks.

POSITIONS

There are believed to be 1025 distinct sexual positions, 50 of which are possibly contrary to the Geneva Convention and hence should not concern us further. (It is also rumoured that there is, in fact, a 1026th position, but the couple who claimed to have invented it have yet to discover a way of regaining their normal posture, and in the meantime this position will be ignored for all practical purposes.) In addition, ten of the positions require planning permission from the local authority, and hence should only be used after seeking professional advice from a chartered surveyor. Some of the more practical positions which might prove of use to the more adventurous reader are as follows:

The missionary position: woman below, man on top, facing each other. (This is the traditional position, but it is, in fact, only one of a whole series of so-called missionary positions, as the examples below illustrate.)

The modern missionary position: man on mission in Africa, woman at home in bed with milkman.

The advanced missionary position: woman below, man on top, facing away from each other.

The evangelistic missionary position: woman below, man at bank cashing in takings.

Puritan missionary position: woman on back, man on front, in separate beds.

American position: woman below, man on top, psychiatrist in between.

Lancashire position: woman below, man in pub.

Polish position: man on top, woman in food queue.

English position: woman below, man waiting to be introduced.

Trade union position: woman below, man negotiating for productivity bonus.

Rear entry (by man): woman below lying face down, man on top also face down.

Rear entry (by woman): man below lying face down, woman on top also lying face down (although providing a good view of the TV for both parties, this position can result in considerable confusion and frustration unless the couple are extraordinarily acrobatic).

Italian position: man in bed, woman in kitchen.

'Perhaps you should have started on something more basic than the Kama Sutra.'

SLOWING THINGS DOWN

Sometimes it is desirable to slow things down a bit, especially if your partner needs more arousal than you do. If you feel you are seriously ahead of your partner there are a number of things you can try to postpone your full ardour:

- close your eyes and think of Salford.
- lower the temperature of the room, or retire to make love in a freezer. (Most reactions slow down with a drop in temperature, the only danger being, of course, that it might slow your partner down even more. There could be a risk of frostbite.)
- sing the national anthem backwards.
- trim your toenails.
- have a cold shower or go for a walk. Tell your partner to carry on without you. (This may sound a little callous.)
- discuss the balance of payments crisis with your partner.
- mentally produce a list of your friends and acquaintances organized on the basis of ascending shoe size.
- watch television.
- check your last bank statement.
- pay a few bills.
- attempt to refute the law of gravity.
- write a corollary to the general theory of relativity.
- order a take-away meal.

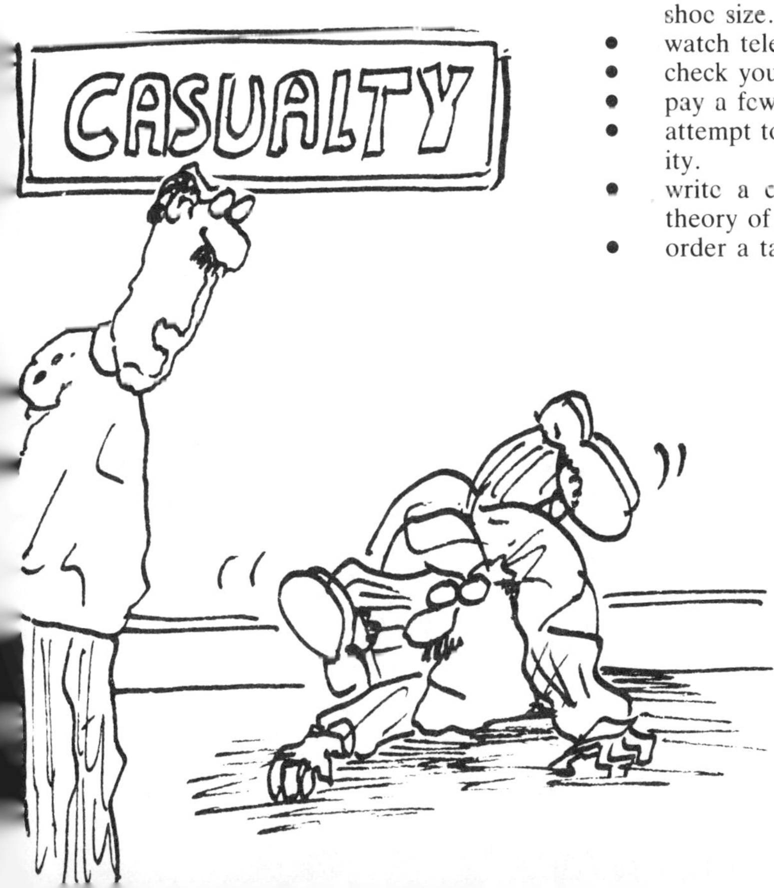

EROGENOUS ZONES

Erogenous zones are parts of the body which, by means of their stimulation, enhance sexual pleaure. There is no definitive list of erogenous zones, as different parts of the body have different effects on different people. We may classify parts of the body according to how frequently they are perceived as erogenous:

Very common erogenous zones:

- the lips
- the tongue
- the breasts
- the buttocks
- the legs
- the thighs
- the hair
- the external genitalia.

Less common erogenous zones:

- the feet
- the navel
- the refrigerator
- the earlobes
- the armpits.

Rare erogenous zones:

- the pancreas
- the hair follicles
- the aorta
- the small intestine
- the islets of Langerhans
- the cerebral cortex
- the tonsils and uvula
- most parts of the lymphatic system.

Generally most people are fairly conservative about erogenous zones, and an easy way to perk up a flagging sex life is to experiment with stimulating some of the less common sites listed above. Also it can add real variety by trying different ways of stimulation beyond the normal stroking, kissing, sucking, etc. For example, miracles can be worked with an over-ripe banana especially when it is aimed at the pancreas; or experiment with the amazing influence of a spicy salami on the soles of the feet or, being really adventurous, on the lymph nodes of the lower trunk. If you are really at a loss for ideas the author has found that throwing an erogenous zone party can be a most rewarding experience.

SHYNESS

Shyness is one of the great handicaps to a really enjoyable sex life. At its worst shyness can be so bad that a person never meets or converses with members of the opposite sex, so that the opportunities for sexual encounters are minimal. Some of the more common manifestations of shyness are as follows:

- making love with socks on.
- keeping shoes and socks on at all times (could on the other hand be a simple footwear fetish).
- making love with a paper bag over your head (with some partners this can be a positive turn-on, especially if you are really ugly).
- remaining fully clothed.
- making love inside a sealed black polythene sack. This can, in fact, be quite dangerous because apart from the obvious risk of suffocation, there is a possibility that the black plastic will stimulate some partners beyond safe limits of arousal.
- remaining in separate beds. Makes sex challenging, to say the least.
- remaining in separate rooms. This makes sex extraordinarily difficult, but correspondingly enjoyable if successful. A lot hinges on the size of the keyhole.
- keeping the light off. This can be fun, but there is the risk of ending up making love to the wrong partner, or even to the pillow if your partner is normally fairly passive.
- using false moustache, beard and wig. A sign of real shyness, especially in women.
- claiming afterwards it was somebody else.

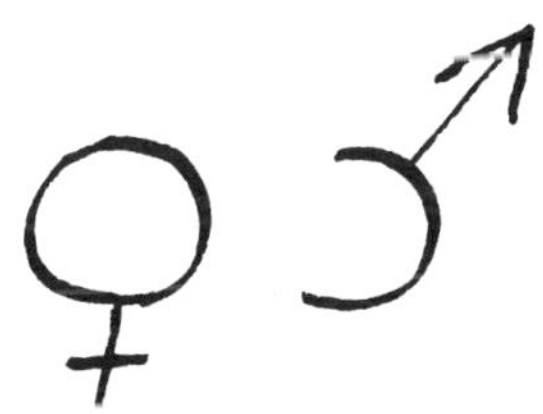

'You're only half the man I married.'

RUINING THE MOOD

Enjoyable and romantic sex requires a certain special mood which can take hours to create. Unfortunately, regardless of how long it took to create the mood, it can so easily be ruined in a matter of seconds by a wrong word or deed. Some partners are more sensitive than others; some are put off sex for life by the minutest shift in the earth's magnetic field, whilst others can cheerfully press on with sex even when the bailiffs are throwing you out of your home, a positive test result for herpes has just come through the post, and you have confessed to being gay. Some of the golden rules to avoid ruining the mood are as follows:

- don't fall out of bed. This can be physically dangerous, as well as rather off-putting, and in some cases distractingly amusing.
- don't fart.
- don't start discussing the economic situation, and whether interest rates are set to rise.
- don't start cutting your toe nails.
- don't start cleaning out your navel.
- don't say half-way through 'I should have had a bath'.
- don't break off to carry the dust-bin out to the road.
- don't chew celery.
- don't pick your nose, ear or any other body orifice unless you can make it look part of the act.
- don't go to get a hot-water bottle.
- don't start discussing what colour to paint the bedroom.
- don't enquire about the price of copper-wire bars on the London metal exchange.
- don't throw up (unless you can do so in a way that your partner won't notice).
- don't say 'I'd give anything for a good steak'.
- don't call your partner by the wrong name (and especially not by a name of the wrong sex, or a name such as Fido which might suggest strange interests).
- don't ask your partner his/her name even if you have forgotten it.

'I'm feeling queer today.'

DISAPPOINTMENT

There are many aspects of sex where severe disappointment can arise; and this is not confined just to performance in bed. The secret is not to let the disappointment really get to you, otherwise a chronic sexual problem can arise. Some of the commonly encountered forms of disappointment are as follows:

- partner laughs at you when you get undressed.
- your partner's physical attributes turn out to be all fake.
- partner turns out to be of the wrong sex.
- partner turns out to be of the wrong species.
- partner looked better with clothes on after all.
- partner leaves half-way through for a hamburger.
- you realize you'd have preferred a hamburger as well.
- loss of erection at a critical stage.
- even worse, there was a loss of erection and neither you nor your partner noticed.
- partner says, 'Was that it?'
- you decide half-way through that cutting the lawn might have been more fun.
- orgasm takes place within the first three seconds.
- orgasm doesn't take place within the first three days.
- in response to an innocent enquiry in the form 'How was it?' your partner responds 'How was what?'
- half-way through your partner opens his/her eyes and says 'Who the blazes are you, and how long have you been here?'
- partner expects payment after the event.
- partner says, 'I could lend you a book about it if you like'.
- partner says, 'Have you seen a psychiatrist about it?' when you don't know what he/she is talking about.
- partner says, 'I wish I were gay' as you are nearing orgasm.
- partner says 'You remind me of my father/mother' after it is all over.
- partner says, 'Well, I suppose you were tired' when you thought you had just redefined the upper limit of sexual performance.

DEALING WITH INTERRUPTIONS

Interruptions are the worst enemy of good sex. Not only can the enjoyment be spoilt, but in the case of the male partner an unexpected intrusion can easily jeopardize his ability to carry on at all. The secret is to know how to deal with interruptions so that they cause the minimum amount of upset; ideally the interruption should be totally ignored, and you should carry on as if nothing had happened. Sometimes this is not possible (for example, if your partner has left), but often with careful training the impact of such interruptions can be kept to a minimum. Below we list some of the more disrupting interruptions, and give some guide as to how they should be dealt with.

The phone rings Ideally the phone should have been taken off the hook beforehand, but if it wasn't and it starts to ring there is no use ignoring it; each ring will knock yet another nail into the coffin of your passion. The best thing to do is answer it without delay and do one of the following:

- say it is the Suzie Wong Massage Parlour
- fart loudly into the mouthpiece (requires some practice)
- start heavy breathing
- say you are a doctor attending your own heart-attack
- claim to be the local vicar
- say 'Emergency, which number do you require?'

Any of these should prompt the caller to hang up smartly. When he or she does, leave your own phone off the hook. Then you are safe.

You both roll off the bed If possible pretend it was deliberate and just carry on on the floor.

Only one of you rolls off the bed Smartly pull your partner after you and exclaim that it's always more fun on the carpet.

The bed collapses If no injury results just carry on, pausing only to compliment your partner on a really spirited performance.

The bed squeaks One of the worst interruptions, purely the result of poor bed maintenance, for which there is no excuse. People have no problem getting their cars serviced regularly, and if you take your sex as seriously as your car then you should check for squeaks or structural problems. It is difficult to do anything about most squeaks, but it is always a good idea to keep an oil gun and a jar of talcum powder handy. Find some good excuse to get out of bed for a few seconds, and smartly try each remedy in turn on the springs. If this doesn't work suggest making love standing up instead.

Your partner is arrested Having the police break in to arrest your partner looks at first glance like a hopeless situation. But try to salvage what you can from it; try for example inviting the police to join in, or say you are a good friend of the Chief Constable, or best of all exclaim surprise that they don't recognize your partner as being the Chief Constable's wife. This should give you enough breathing space to finish off the job in hand and help your partner make a getaway.

Your partner turns gay part way through There is no easy answer to this one, and it may be wise to keep a spare partner within three minutes' travelling time.

Your partner gets an uncontrollable hiccuping fit The only speedy cure is a sudden surprise. A very loud 'Boo!!' or bursting a paper bag normally works, but this can put your partner off sex for a good few minutes.

Your husband/wife walks in A difficult one, this. First, try saying, 'We've been waiting for you', and if he/she joins in without complaint all is well. If this doesn't work an attack of amnesia may be the best bet: just say, 'Who are you?'. This is likely to give you at least a few minutes' breathing space to think of a plausible defence.

Partner cannot remember where the whip/vibrator/vinyl stockings/leather thongs are kept There is no easy answer here; it merely demonstrates the need for careful planning.

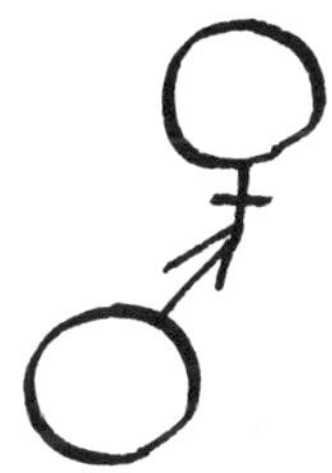

'Is it true you used to work in a circus?'

THINGS TO DO DURING SEX

Sex can, in fact, be quite a boring pastime. If your partner is one who requires a considerable amount of pre-sex stimulation (for example, one to two hours of good solid foreplay), or your whole sexual style is low-key, and makes little use of the hands, mouth or brain, you may find time hanging rather heavily after a while. Some dedicated lovers believe that prolonged sex expands and elevates the supreme pinnacle of the conscious mind until the id, the ego, the soul and all south-facing sweat glands enter a state of superficial hyper-anti-regressive transcendental harmony in which, from a purely psycho-socio-religious standpoint, the spirit, the subconscious, the hair follicles in the groin and the entire endocrine system become, in effect, one. Such lovers are in a minority; most, after the first hour, are basically bored. In order to avert such boredom putting you off the whole idea of sex, it is advisable to apply your mind to some more challenging task. Below we give some examples of suitable brain-engaging activities:

- from memory alone reorganize the entire US Library of Congress on the basis of the authors' inside-leg measurements. In addition to being mentally challenging, it can also be very hard work if a substantial portion of the measurement is to be undertaken by the individual concerned.
- refute the law of gravity. Apart from being an excellent way of occupying the brain during prolonged sex sessions, this could well bring added benefits by way of Nobel Prizes, knighthoods, great wealth, and guest appearances on the Terry Wogan and Johnnie Carson Shows. However, if successful, it could introduce unforeseen problems in the sexual arena due to loss of all meaningful weight.
- discover a new physical dimension.
- ponder on the fundamental incompatibility between modern current cost accounting standards and recent advances in the treatment of fungal infections of the scalp.
- train as a chartered accountant. This has the advantage of being somewhat less challenging than the other activities mentioned here (or indeed most activities generally except, perhaps, ageing or growing your toe nails).
- translate from the original Braille into Serbo-Croat Max von Lehrstein's *Nasal Secretions and 101 Other Really Interesting Things*.
- establish beyond all reasonable doubt that electro-magnetic forces actually originate from the gents' cloakroom of Orpington and Sevenoaks British Legion Club. This activity should amply tax even the most bored of lovers' minds, but would if successful revolutionize modern physics as well as boosting Legion membership to record levels. It would also lead to a fundamental redefinition of magnetic north and reduce the Arctic region to the status of a rather boring and cold area north of Watford.
- think up a good explanation for why you are not at that sales conference in Harrogate.
- think up a gentle way of suggesting that you'd really like things speeded up a bit next time.

'A third sex, eh . . .'

THINGS TO TALK ABOUT DURING THE TIME LEADING UP TO ORGASM

If your partner is one of those people who takes a particuarly long time to arouse, or enjoys particularly prolonged orgasms (for example, in excess of three-and-a-half hours), you may begin to find the time weighing rather heavily on your mind, and you may find that indulging in some innocent conversation helps obviate the risk of boredom. At such a sensitive time, however, you must choose the topic for such conversation with the greatest care. Examples of good and bad topics are given below:

Good Topics
- the aesthetic beauty of fresh young daffodils gently swaying in a spring breeze.
- the glow of the autumn sunset over San Francisco Bay.
- the distant sound of surf breaking on a quiet golden beach in a remote corner of Tahiti.
- the golden glow of a Chiltern beechwood in the weak sun of a late October afternoon.
- the soul-etching freshness of a tropical rainstorm on a hot humid afternoon in the steamy jungle of Sumatra.

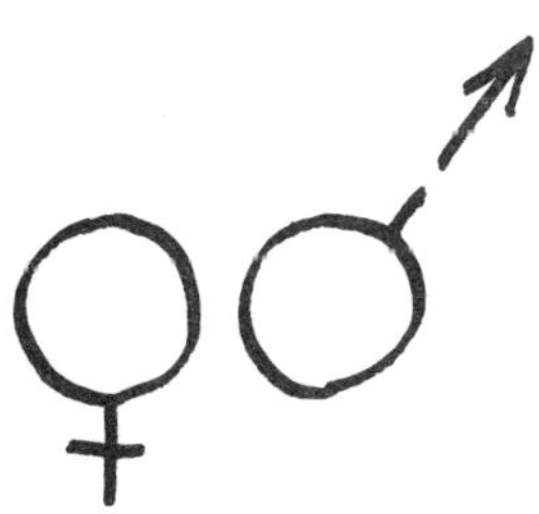

'Is it true you've had a vasectomy?'

Bad Topics
- design standards for 2-foot sewage outfall pipes.
- fungal infections of the foot.
- the marginal fiscal impact of ergot infestation in the barley crop in the East Shetlands in the late nineteenth century.
- the relative merits of 20/30W and 20/50W lubricants for V12 twin-cam production petrol engines with swept capacity in excess of 4 litres.
- whether man, by virtue of his existence and the promotional activity of deodorant manufacturers, is latently gay in character.
- whether Einstein and Percy Wyndham Lewis were one and the same (or 0.99999999999999999999999997 and the same at a measured velocity of 2.5 mph).

(All of these latter topics, whilst none the less virtuous subjects for discussion at the appropriate time, suggest a certain insensitivity and lack of feeling during love-making.)

ORGASM

Technically speaking (with acknowledgements to the *Oxford English Dictionary*) an orgasm is ' . . . an immoderate action or excitement, a paroxysm of desire or rage or other passion'. Clearly not all orgasms are strictly sexual in nature; many immoderate actions, such as sticking a parking ticket to a car windscreen have little or nothing to do with the bedroom, unless of course you happen to be married to the traffic warden concerned in which case a paroxysm of rage may well be the only orgasm which results.

Within the more limited sexual context of orgasms there is still an enormous range of different phenomena which may be described by the word. Sexual orgasms range from events little more spectacular and earth-shattering than a sneeze to apocalyptic happenings embracing all the excitement of an eruption of Krakatoa, a sunset over the South China Sea, man's first landing on the moon, a 10-megaton nuclear explosion and a Democratic Primary in Connecticut. The intensity of an orgasm is usually measured on a 12-point scale devised by the same Admiral Sir Francis Beaufort who is famous for wind-speed measurement; he discovered eventually that there is more to life than just meteorology. This scale relates the orgasm to its effect on the environment, in the following way:

'Phew, that was quite a night!'

Beaufort Scale of Orgasmic Intensity

BEAUFORT NUMBER	ORGASM	EFFECT ON THE ENVIRONMENT
0	No orgasm	No visible emotion or movement.
1	Slight orgasm	Slight facial emotion, no visible movement or noise.
2	Mild orgasm	Considerable facial expression, slight sighing or moaning.
3	Moderate orgasm	Moaning and sighing, slight writhing movements.
4	Full orgasm	Strong moaning, considerable body movement. Some sweating.
5	Strong orgasm	Bed shakes, floorboards creak. Strong moaning, bodies sweat and take on flushed appearance.
6	Very strong orgasm	Bed may move across room. Risk of damage to skin and clothing.
7	Severe orgasm	Bed may leave the floor for extended periods. Damage to bed-clothes. Considerable embarrassment to people in neighbouring rooms.
8	Very severe orgasm	House vibrates strongly. Loose tiles may be displaced. Felt by neighbours and heard outside on quiet nights.
9	Cataclysmic orgasm	Severe damage to bed. Floorboards uprooted. Risk of secondary damage to furniture in same room. Neighbours disturbed even when asleep.
10	Devastating orgasm	Severe damage to bedroom. Light fitting torn from ceiling. Windows shattered. Neighbours petition for peace and quiet.
11	Storm-force orgasm	Trees uprooted. Moderate structural damage to houses. Risk of severe injury.
12	Hurricane-force orgasm	Severe structural damage to houses. Little vegetation left standing. Risk of loss of life.

The ideal orgasm is believed to lie within the range 3–7. Anything below this on the scale is likely to be a severe disappointment, whilst anything over 7 can prove expensive and risky. In the author's personal experience 5 is a good average, with a 6 or 7 about once every 6 weeks. (People living in bungalows may safely average 6 or 7, whilst unfortunate flat-dwellers are advised to limit themselves to an average of 4, unless they have particularly broad-minded neighbours. Out of doors no such limitations need apply, and so long as there is no risk of low-flying aircraft the full range of the scale may be safely explored.)

TYPES OF ORGASM

In the male of the species an orgasm is an orgasm is an orgasm; for the male population it is difficult to distinguish one orgasm from another, except to say that one was, say, 10 per cent more earth shattering than another. In the case of the female, however, the situation is quite different. In a recent piece of research (for which the author thanks a rather tired friend) 2098 different types of female orgasm were identified of which 56 required the use of scaffolding or a pair of strong ladders, 32 are likely to result in permanent injury to the endocrine system, 45 can only be experienced underwater, and 15 are likely to attract Value Added Tax. Of the remaining 1950 the following examples may be of special interest to the reader:

The clitoral orgasm: the most intense of all, but short-lived.

The vaginal orgasm: deeper, more gentle but longer and in many cases more satisfying.

The oral orgasm: often the result of eating a Mars bar too quickly.

The aural orgasm: relatively rare, and sometimes the result of highly inaccurate penetration by short-sighted lovers.

The nasal orgasm: often mistaken for a sneeze, but definitely to be avoided in cases of colds or 'flu.

The tonsular orgasm: usually the result of eating a 3-pack of Mars bars in one go without removing the wrappers.

The cerebral orgasm: the ultimate pinnacle of orgasmic experience when each individual brain cell pulsates like a Belisha beacon.

HOW TO TELL IF YOUR PARTNER HAS HAD AN ORGASM

Many people are very concerned to know whether their partner has actually had an orgasm or not. If your partner is not one of the more extrovert sorts who laugh, scream, yell, write poetry or put an announcement in *The Times*, then this can be really quite difficult. There are many methods used to establish a partner's orgasmic state, some of which are more tactful than others. Among the techniques which have come to the author's attention are:

- asking your parter straight out. This is simple and quick, but puts many people off. It tends to suggest boredom or impatience.
- asking your partner in a more roundabout way. For example, by saying. 'If, purely theoretically, I were to enquire about your contemporary orgasmic experience attainment situation condition, would you be pre-disposed to respond in the affirmative?' Although less blunt and direct than the first approach, there is a serious risk that your partner will not understand a single word.
- formal cross-examination under oath. This suggests a lack of trust rather out of line with the whole concept of love-making, and is not recommended.
- write your partner a letter. Much less blunt than asking directly and you can always disguise the question in flowery, romantic verse. Good for partners who come very slowly, but use a first-class stamp unless your partner is one of the few who require a good few days of dedicated foreplay to get really in the mood.
- send a telex. Quicker than a letter, but often appears a bit too business-like.
- telephone. A nice way to enquire, but only really any good in bedrooms with two independent outside lines.
- place a notice in the personal column of the local newspaper. Pleasantly indirect, but a bit too public for most partners.
- get a friend to ask for you. This can be real fun, especially if the friend is willing to enter fully into the spirit of the occasion. Not recommended with shy partners.
- just keep going long enough to make sure. After the first two days of solid love-making it is usually safe to assume your partner must have had at least one orgasm.
- consult a clairvoyant. May be a bit off-putting and distracting. There is a severe risk of ruining the mood, especially if the clairvoyant lives more than a few doors away.
- examine the bed for structural damage. This comes under the general heading of retrospective tests, and may only give a reliable guide in the case of really frisky partners.
- invent, patent, manufacture, market and then use an orgasmeter. This is one of the more original suggestions put to the author, and although very slow and time-consuming it may help prevent premature ejaculation (because of the mental concentration required) and there is a good chance of qualifying for a government grant.

The alternative solution is, of course, to get rid of the common hang-up about sex only being enjoyable if you succeed in reaching the orgasmic state. The more relaxed the two partners are, the more likely the whole event is to be enjoyable. Indeed recent research has shown that while herring rarely exhibit the symptoms of orgasm, there is no evidence that on average they are less satisfied with their sex lives than most adult human beings.

HOW TO TELL IF YOU YOURSELF HAVE HAD AN ORGASM

While many people may experience difficulty in telling whether an introverted partner has had an orgasm, some really shy people suffer a more fundamental problem of trying to establish whether they themselves have had an orgasm or not. There are several ways in which they may attempt to establish their orgasmic state:

- ask themselves. If the person involved is exceptionally shy there is of course the risk that they may ignore themselves, or even lie to conceal the truth.
- write themselves a letter. Really shy people may find it easier to be straightforward and honest with themselves in writing.
- look. This is not easy unless they know exactly what they are looking for.
- check their pulse rate, heart rate and blood pressure. All these are likely to be elevated post-orgasmically. However, in order to establish whether they are higher than normal it may prove necessary continuously to monitor all three body functions, and in practice the equipment involved may put off even the most loving and broad-minded partner.
- ask your partner if he or she thinks you have had an orgasm.
- seek expert medical advice.
- ask a chartered surveyor.
- guess. At least you are likely to be exactly right 50 per cent of the time.

'You've been drinking again.'

FAILURE TO ACHIEVE ORGASM

At some time in their lives most people will have some difficulty achieving an orgasm. Many people take this as a sign of failure and worry about it; this is really quite unnecessary, and only tends to make the problem worse. In practice such episodes quickly pass, and the sex life returns rapidly to normal. Some of the more common reasons for failing to reach a climax are as follows:

- partner not really in the mood.
- insufficient effort and attention to foreplay.
- exhaustion.
- worry, especially about work and money.
- you don't really fancy your partner that much.
- partner wrong sex.
- partner too far away (in practice it is difficult to achieve a really satisfying orgasm if your partner is more than three feet away).
- too many people looking on.
- distraction by radio, TV, studio lights, etc.
- worry that somebody might come into the room (especially your partner's spouse).
- too much alcohol (it may be difficult to manage sex of any sort if you are too drunk).
- too little alcohol.
- partner is snoring too loudly.
- partner has just confessed to being gay.
- partner has just confessed to being a CIA agent sent to spy on you.
- worry that your partner has just confessed to being gay but you don't even seem to mind.
- the bed has just collapsed.

'It's just post-natal depression.'

IMPOTENCE AND FRIGIDITY

'I'm not off sex . . . I've merely entered the preliminary phase of a transient libido reduction situation condition.'

There will be times in most people's lives when they discover, at the critical moment, that they are not really in the mood for sex and find it difficult to carry on. In women this problem is called frigidity, while in men the most common symptom is impotence. In this area of sex women have a slight advantage. A woman can at least moan, writhe and scream for sex, sex, sex . . . even though she is really longing to do the ironing or read a good book. Men on the other hand experience not only the psychological symptoms but also certain mechanical limitations which make it rather difficult to pretend; a man may sound convincing if he moans, writhes and screams for sex, but if his organ is as stiff as yesterday's lettuce the pretence is likely to be short-lived. Frigidity and impotence have many causes, principal amongst which are the following:

Causes of Impotence

- fear of failure. This creates a vicious circle where the impotence makes the fear worse, and the fear makes the impotence worse. Often the man forgets what he was afraid of and is just left with the impotence.
- your partner starts to talk about her husband.
- you find you are too intellectual for mundane physical sex.
- you are gay.
- senility (impotence is common in the over-95s).
- fear of traffic wardens. This is common when you only put enough money in the meter for a quick session, but the foreplay is about to enter its second hour.
- you start to worry whether she might ask you to pay.
- you have been set a rigid time limit, such as 5 minutes 25 seconds.
- you have been set a limit of 45 thrusts only.
- you have had too much to drink and the room won't keep still.
- you notice she bears an uncanny resemblance to your mother.
- there are too many people watching.
- the cine-camera makes too much noise.
- the tent has just blown over.
- you realize you have forgotten to draw the curtains.
- your partner has just told you that you will be scored out of 10.
- you suddenly catch sight of a special clinic appointment card on the bedside locker.
- she says you are nearly as good in bed as Luton Football Club.
- you have a deep-rooted fear of catching a nasty disease.
- your organ is genuinely worn out.
- you don't fancy your partner.
- partner is the wrong sex.
- partner is the wrong species.

Causes of Frigidity

- partner looks like father.
- partner looks like mother.
- partner wears corrective underwear.
- partner's wig keeps sliding off on to your face.
- partner keeps asking how you are doing.
- partner asks you how long it will take because there's a match on TV in 15 minutes' time.
- you are hungry and even your partner starts to look edible.
- you partner's medallion keeps bashing you on the nose.
- your partner spills his beer down your front.
- you are worrying about your children's schooling.
- you are worrying about your own schooling (younger readers only).
- partner wrong sex.
- you can't tell what sex your partner is and this bugs you.
- you just don't fancy him.
- partner keeps looking at clock.
- partner keeps phoning up psychiatrist to explain what's going on.
- money worries.
- partner just called you by the wrong name.
- partner just called you John.

'They say you're a bit of an introvert.'

WHAT TO DO AFTERWARDS

After sex you should, ideally, just bask in the rosy after-glow. If, however, you haven't got an after-glow, never mind a rosy one, or if you find basking just a bit too boring, then you might consider indulging in some suitable bed-based post-coital activity. You should choose such an activity carefully since the post-coital period is, emotionally, quite a sensitive time, and the wrong choice can seriously alienate your partner and give them the impression that you lack true feeling. Below we list some of the good and some of the bad ways of filling the time.

Good Post-coital Activities:

- singing softly.
- playing the guitar.
- quietly sipping a glass of chilled rosé wine.
- sleeping.
- composing a poem to your loved one (OK so long as you don't let your partner know the identity of your loved one).
- eating sun-kissed grapes.

Bad Post-coital Activities:

- completing a VAT return.
- phoning your mother to report on what it was like.
- phoning your wife or husband to say you'll be home soon.
- brass rubbing.
- biting your toe nails.
- eating over-ripe mangoes.
- plucking a chicken.
- ironing (OK in itself, but not good in bed. There are serious risks of scorching).
- writing your next alimony cheque.
- picking your nose or ears. While a discreet and quick poke is not too offensive, a really good mining session lasting 15 minutes or more can be quite off-putting. The same applies to cleaning out your navel, or any other normally hidden body orifice.

FREQUENCY OF SEX

The frequency of sexual activity varies enormously from individual to individual. On average the sexually active male makes love 2.3 times every week. (Research has shown that he enjoys the 2 times much more than the 0.3 times.) There are no golden rules about how often you should indulge in sexual activity, although it is clear that if it is too frequent (for example, more than 5 times an hour) it tends to interfere with normal day-to-day tasks such as working, shopping, eating, etc. and biological needs like sleeping. On the other hand it is desirable that sex is not so infrequent that you forget what to do in between times. In other words, it is desirable to keep your hand in, but not to wear yourself out. Of course, the basic appetite for sex varies from person to person. Some people make love just once a year, and spend the intervening time looking tired and debauched, slowly building up their energy for the next time; while some do it every minute of the day and night and hang around for the other 59 seconds looking bored and getting increasingly frustrated.

Among that part of the population who indulge in more sex than average the main reasons for doing so are:

- poor memory (they cannot remember the last time, and so do it again).
- poverty. It is a cheap way of keeping warm.
- they are wanted by the police. Sex is a good way of avoiding arrest, as it takes an exceptionally tactless and heartless constable to arrest you while making love.
- they just like sex a lot.
- they cannot think of anything better to do.
- they believe it prolongs life.
- they believe it helps the balance of payments situation. (This belief has some validity since if you stay in bed you have little opportunity to import foreign goods.)
- they believe it stops you going bald. (In practice although it may not prevent baldness it certainly helps you to stop worrying about it.)

FETISHES

Technically, a fetish is an object or image superstitiously invested with divine or demonic power, and as such devoutly revered. It derives from the Portuguese word meaning magic. This is not of course what most people think of as a fetish.

In the sexual context a fetish has come to mean an object or ritual of some sort without which sexual excitement and orgasm is not possible. Most people have fetishes of some sort or other, but to only a mild degree; for example black stockings, black underwear, long hair, satin bedclothes. One step further along we get people who like leather, whips, plastic macs, etc. In practice a fetish is only really a problem if it is:

inconvenient: such as the *QEII* or the Eiffel Tower.
impractical: Pacific Ocean, Niagara Falls, a rhinoceros, etc.
expensive: gold-plated underwear, making love on caviar, etc.
embarrassing: sweaty armpits, or an audience of bishops.
illegal: arson, treason, etc.
dangerous: e.g. involving the national grid or flying Boeing 747.
impossible: involving physical movement in 4 dimensions, etc.

In fact most fetishes are quite innocent and harmless, and can add real enjoyment and interest to sex. Any reader who does not already have a suitable fetish, but would like to experiment with one, can try using the random fetish generator shown on the following page. To produce a random fetish all you have to do is select two adjectives and one noun from the flow charts. First look at the part of the diagram labelled 'Adjective Number One' and answer the simple questions until you narrow down your choice to one of the groups of six. Then make a selection at random by rolling a die. Then repeat the procedure to select a second adjective and a noun using the other two charts. This will give you a random fetish from a possible list of 19440. Once you have selected your fetish go ahead and enjoy it to the full. When its effectiveness begins to wane, simply select a replacement for it. The range of fetishes available from these diagrams should keep the average adult happy for many years.

'I've heard of some weird fetishes but this takes the cake!'

ADJECTIVE NUMBER ONE

Do you like things

- that move
  1. squirming
  2. rippling
  3. pulsating
  4. vibrating
  5. writhing
  6. trembling
- that feel
  - wet
    1. dewy
    2. clammy
    3. damp
    4. greasy
    5. oily
    6. moist
  - dry
    1. gritty
    2. rough
    3. weather-beaten
    4. shaggy
    5. bristling
    6. sharp
- that have interesting shapes
  1. undulating
  2. curvy
  3. rounded
  4. oblate
  5. elongated
  6. pendulous
- that sound plain naughty
  1. erotic
  2. pubile
  3. gonadic
  4. ejaculatory
  5. dildolic
  6. orgasmic
- that sound weird
  1. Euclidean
  2. ferriagic
  3. orthogonal
  4. edentate
  5. real weird
  6. logarithmic

ADJECTIVE NUMBER TWO

Do you like things that are

- colourful
  - and pretty
    1. dawn pink
    2. pale lilac
    3. rose red
    4. primrose yellow
    5. autumn gold
    6. midnight blue
  - and plain
    1. red
    2. blue
    3. black
    4. white
    5. green
    6. yellow
  - and putrid
    1. vomit pink
    2. bile yellow
    3. dysentery brown
    4. fetid grey
    5. slime green
    6. gangrene black
- provacative sounding
  1. nude
  2. Swedish
  3. see-through
  4. clinging
  5. erectile
  6. full-frontal
- made of interesting materials
  1. rubber
  2. leather
  3. fur
  4. suede
  5. vinyl
  6. velvet

THE NOUN

Do you like things that are

- soft
  - and edible
    1. ice cream
    2. cream doughnut
    3. cucumber
    4. Mars bar
    5. sausage roll
    6. purgative
  - and inedible
    1. British Rail sandwich
    2. pillow
    3. corset
    4. feather duster
    5. school mistress
    6. gym slip
- hard
  1. Porsche 928
  2. riding boot
  3. cruise missile
  4. vibrator
  5. whip
  6. dentist's surgery

FANTASIES

Many people tolerate an otherwise boring sex life by fantasizing, that is creating an artificial mental image of their mate or their surroundings which sexually arouses them. In around 99 per cent of cases fantasies are quite harmless, and definitely improve sexual enjoyment. Most sexual fantasies fall into one of the following main categories:

Food fantasies: such as making love to an enormous profiterole, or wallowing with 14 naked dusky maidens in a swimming pool full of whipped double cream.

Porsche 928 fantasies: such as making love in the back seat of a Porsche 928, or making love in the front seat of a Porsche 928, or making love in the boot of a Porsche 928, or making love underneath a Porsche 928, or making love to a Porsche 928 salesman, or making love to someone who lives next door to someone who once test-drove a Porsche 928.

Bondage/flagellation fantasies: such as being whipped by six Anglican bishops, or being strapped to the side of the *QEII* and being ravished by the US 6th fleet, or being thrown to a ring full of starving Sumo wrestlers while lashed to a giant French loaf by 56 feet of cooked spaghetti.

Very practical or mundane fantasies: such as making love on the other side of the bed to normal, or doing it with Mrs Smith from No. 14, or making love during *Coronation Street.*

Celebrity fantasies: a free-for-all with Joan Collins/Robert Redford (depending on your sex, or both if you are game for anything), or being carried off by King Kong or Godzilla.

Money fantasies: such as rolling around on a bed of $1000 bills, or being paid to spend the night with fifteen insomniac nymphomaniac starlets trying to break into Hollywood, who think you are Steven Spielberg.

Location/situation fantasies: such as making love on the top of the Eiffel Tower, making love to the Eiffel Tower, doing it in a small boat shooting Niagara Falls, being dragged into the desert by a dark and dashing cost accountant named Aubrey, etc.

Object fantasies: making love to a trombone, cuddling Mount Everest, doing really naughty things with a Mars 3-pack, etc.

'You were OK, but the rugby team was better.'

GROUP SEX

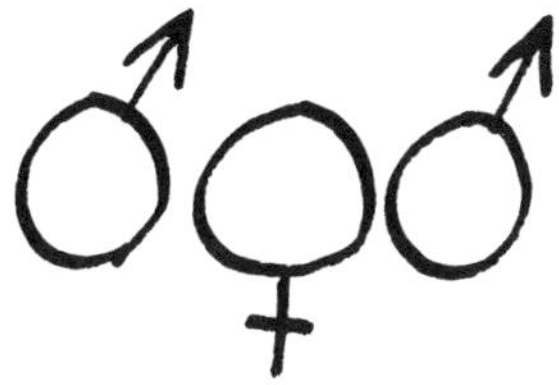

'I'm not that sort of girl.'

Technically speaking, all sex which involves more than one person is group sex. However, the term is normally used to refer to sexual activity involving at least three people, and often more (reports of orgies involving in excess of 15,000 people are probably exaggerated, but groups of between 6 and 10 are believed to be quite common, particularly in the Milton Keynes area; this is understandable as there is actually very little else to do in Milton Keynes). Group sex, as opposed to pair-wise sex, has both advantages and disadvantages, the principal amongst which are:

Advantages:

- it offers more variety.
- you are more likely, at any instant in time, to find someone who is in the mood.
- it can be a good way to meet people if you are new to the area.
- in a group less interruption is caused if one individual wishes to break off to go to the loo, make a sandwich, watch *Match of the Day*, or make up a four for bridge.
- it can be a good way of saving on heating bills.
- it can create something of a carnival atmosphere.
- you can inject interest by holding little competitions, such as a prize for the fastest orgasm, or the most original position.

Disadvantages:

- you need a large bed or at least very slim partners.
- shyness may be a problem at first.
- you may be spoilt for choice.
- unnecessary competitiveness may emerge.
- it may all become rather noisy.
- the group may end up consuming vast amounts of food and drink.
- you may need to strengthen the floors of your house or flat to take the extra weight.
- it it happens regularly you may become liable to pay the participants' national insurance contributions.
- in the heat of the moment you may confuse the sexes and end up being rather embarrassed.
- it may take a lot of time to introduce yourselves and shake hands.
- your clothes may get mixed up if not labelled clearly.
- the parentage of any resulting offspring may be ambiguous.

SOME INTERESTING STATISTICS

Over the years many books have been published which present various statistics about interesting aspects of sex; the work of Kinsey is of particular interest. However, certain areas have not been well covered in existing publications, and in an attempt to put the record straight, as it were, we present below some statistics on the more neglected aspects of sexual activity.

- 99.999 per cent of sexual partners know each other's first name at the outset of the sexual activity. Of the remaining 0.001 per cent, 25 per cent do not have a first name to know, while 92 per cent of the other 75 per cent know each other's first name once sexual activity has been completed. Half of the remaining 8 per cent of the 75 per cent who did have a first name, but who were unaware of it before sexual activity started, thought their partner was called Cumming (presumably because the only intelligible words uttered were 'I'm coming!!') whilst 40 per cent of the other half of the 75 per cent who did have a first name to know but who were unaware of it before sexual activity started learned their partner's first name during sex but had forgotten it by the time it was completed (normally due to impacting their head on the wall at a particularly spirited moment). Interestingly, 32 per cent of the 60 per cent of the other half of the 75 per cent who did have a first name to know but were unaware of it before sexual activity, couldn't remember whether or not they had remembered their partner's name during sex and then forgotten it, or whether they had consistently not remembered it throughout. Sex is one activity often associated with poor memories (for example, forgetting whether one is married or not).

- The average sexually active adult has a total of 4.5 sexual partners between the ages of 20 and 60. However, 99.9 per cent of people say sex was more satisfying with the four partners than with the 0.5 partner. Only small numbers of people (<0.000001 per cent) have more than 158 partners, whilst an even smaller number (<0.00000001 per cent) have less than 0.8 partners.

- 92 per cent of people are sexually active by the age of 25 and remain sexually active until the age of 55. However, 99.99999 per cent take some form of rest in the intervening 30 years, and in more than 99.99 per cent of cases this rest is of more than 4 minutes' duration.

- When asked to describe in one word their most recent sexual experience 96 per cent of people use long words with at least three syllables (e.g. shattering, unbelievable, fantastic, incredible, neanderthal, intergalactic, wonderful,

etc.) when the sex was good, and short words of just one or two syllables (e.g. quick, cheap, wet, stale, slack, woody, yuk, etc.) when the sex was bad. This suggests some evolutionary link between inter-sex down-time and the quality of sex; in other words when the experience was good extra time is spent chatting to ensure that subsequent copulations are sufficiently infrequent to guarantee no devaluation of the pleasure. Alternatively it might suggest something totally different. In any case it does indicate that good-quality sex enhances a person's active vocabulary, which is as good as any excuse.

- sex is actually a three-letter word. In order to be a four-letter word, and thereby rank as being rude, it would have to be spelt as 'sekx', but then nobody would know what you were talking about. Hence, by its very nature, sex is not rude.

MALE ORGAN SIZE

'I can tell you're pleased to see me!'

It has now been widely recognized for a number of years that the sheer physical size of the male sex organ has little bearing upon sexual performance and enjoyment. (The exceptions to this otherwise golden rule arise when the organ is either so large that it needs the whole bed to itself or so small that a prolonged search is required to locate it at all.) Other things being equal, a small item of equipment used well can knock the spots off its badly managed larger cousin. Lack of size can be so easily compensated for by superior technique or just honest to goodness down-to-earth enthusiasm. Also, in addition to size, so many other factors such as texture, colour, and shape can compensate for lack of stature; if a gentleman is lucky enough to have a square, furry, bright blue organ then the world (or at least all the feminine half, and, if we believe published statistics, around 15–20 per cent of the male half) is his oyster.

In order to rate the male organ for performance we need to take into account all these relevant features, and the author is indebted to sources who prefer to remain anonymous for the following index:

Male Organ Performance Index (MOPI)

100	+ 2 ×	the erect length in cms
	+ 1 ×	the flaccid length in cms
	+ 3 ×	the maximum erect circumference in cms (adding 50 points if the process of measurement brought on an instant orgasm)
	+ 4 ×	the peak sustainable thrust rate in beats per minute
	+ 3 ×	the maximum acceleration rate in cm per sec
	− 4 ×	the reduction in peak thrust rate after second orgasm
	− 5 ×	number of seconds taken for emergency stop
	− 6 ×	number of seconds taken for emergency withdrawal
	− 4 ×	number of minutes of 'down time' between orgasms

To this basic score are added the following possible bonus points:

100	for corrugated finish
75	for fluorescence
50	for unusual colour (e.g., green or purple with pink spots)
40	for a floral pattern
25	for a furry or velvety surface
56	for an in-built vibrator
10	for a clear vasectomy scar

If more than one organ is possessed then the scores are cumulative, but a further 500 points are added for novelty value.

Regression analysis has shown that this index is capable of predicting sexual satisfaction before the event to within 5 per cent confidence at least 85 per cent of the time. It is also apparent that qualified statisticians significantly enjoy sex more than non-qualified statisticians, as they are the only ones who actually know how to use the measure.

On this scale the value of the Male Organ Performance Index may range between −258 and +6290*. The 'normal' range is thought to be between 250 and 320.

*The author's contact was busy investigating a reported score in excess of this at the time of publication, but has yet to report back with any reliable score; the only communications so far have been moans, sighs and faintly uttered words which sounded like 'wow!'.

'It happens to every man sometimes.'

SEX-RELATED INJURIES

Sex is in fact a very hazardous activity, and casualty wards up and down the country are often asked to repair the very considerable damage which may result when things get a bit too spirited or out of hand. The most common sex-related injuries are:

Whiplash injuries to the neck, often caused in the 15 seconds prior to orgasm.

Scorched knees and scorched elbows, usually the result of rough or unsuitable bedclothes or making love on rush matting.

Abrasion of the chin, nose and earlobes this is usually in advanced sexual positions.

Torsion of the testicles A painful condition resulting from really strenuous movement with an unsupported scrotum.

Torsion of the sweat glands. The result of even more frantic love-making, especially in warm weather.

Concussion Commonly caused by having an insufficient gap between the bed and the wall.

Sprains, especially of the wrist, ankle, knee, elbow and other parts of the body used for support during sex. Less common sprains are seen in the eyebrows, tonsils, and vocal cords (the usual result of really spirited moaning).

Indigestion Most frequently the result of trying to eat during sex. Often can be so severe as to require hospitalization.

Brain damage Sometimes caused by trying to think during sex, or interpret the detailed instructions of a sex manual when things have already started to warm up.

Heart failure The result of trying too much, too soon, with too many different people.

Amnesia The reason why many men forget they are married.

Skin punctures Usually by fingernails, but sometimes by other objects used during sex such as knives, whips, bottles, fork-lift trucks, video cameras, rugby boots, etc.

Tooth decay Although the causal link has not been established, it is interesting to note that of all caries sufferers over 60 per cent are sexually active.

Death Often the result of making some dreadful confession just prior to the moment of orgasm (such as 'I'm your brother', 'I'm really a donkey', or 'Have you been on TV before?').

Accidental castration, and the lesser form of injury, zipped scrotum. A common injury caused by attempting to put trousers back on too quickly. Sometimes occurs too when partner attempts to remove your trousers without first removing large dress rings.

Baldness Although normally thought to be purely hereditary, it is now known that much baldness is caused in bed either through excessive friction on the

'It must have been some love-bite.'

scalp or through hair being pulled out by over-excited partner.

Impacted penis Usually caused by falling out of bed at the wrong time. Can be extremely unpleasant. Thought to be the reason why many men like to make love on the floor.

Injuries due to foreign bodies During sex many people use various aids which may get stuck and hence cause distress and injury. Common problems involve bottles, candles, tight rings, harpsichords, hydraulic jacks, whip handles, Porsche 928 camshafts, watering cans, candy bars, various leguminous vegetables and pieces of Lego.

AVOIDING PREGNANCY

One of the natural by-products of sex is pregnancy, and if this condition is to be avoided some active measure must be taken to prevent it. This is what contraception is all about. Most people take a fairly narrow view of contraception, and think only in terms of the pill, the sheath, the coil, etc. In practice contraception is a much wider issue than this. Basically there are three different types of contraception, as the following examples show:

Contraception by Making Sex Impossible

- joining a celibate order of monks.
- by jogging 24 hours a day (strictly speaking sex while jogging is not totally impossible, but it is sufficiently difficult to find a partner adept enough at jogging backwards at the same speed as yourself to warrant its inclusion under this heading).
- making love only when there's a K in the month (this is an advanced version of the rhythm method).
- surgical removal of all external genitalia (a trifle too drastic in most instances).
- excess alcohol. Whilst alcohol in moderation can be a definite aphrodisiac, in excess (e.g., more than five bottles of wine, 32 measures of spirits, or 18 pints of beer) it makes sex extremely difficult or even impossible. In the case of the measure of beer sex is usually rendered impossible by virtue of there being insufficient time available between successive visits to the lavatory.

Contraception by Making Sex Extremely Difficult

- living with your in-laws. One of the most effective ways of making sex extremely difficult is to know that your mother-in law is sleeping in the next room with her ear to the wall.
- only making love during a free-fall parachute jump.
- by joining the Civil Service or working in local government. Under such circumstances the person concerned is likely to become too boring to make anyone pregnant; and in any case pregnancy is probably only permitted with the written consent of a Permanent Under-Secretary.
- by becoming gay.
- by making love only inside a Porsche 928. While this is an extremely effective form of contraception it has the added advantage that almost anything done inside, on top of, underneath or anywhere near a Porsche 928 is fun.

Contraception by Making Sex Unproductive

- by mating only with animals of a different species.
- by using any of the well-established techniques such as the Pill, the coil, the sheath, spermicidal sprays (soon, it is believed, to be outlawed by the Spermatazoa Liberation Front).
- by making love only to inanimate objects (inflatable dolls, your pillow, a Porsche 928 etc.).
- coitus interruptus (otherwise known as taking a commercial break).
- coitus obstructus (i.e., sleeping in different rooms separated by a door with an extremely small key-hole).
- vasectomy.
- by mating in the wrong way (e.g., by using the wrong orifice, such as the navel, the ear, the nostrils, the tear duct or any part of the lymphatic or endocrine systems).

'I've got news for you.'

'If you must know, it's the patron saint of headaches.'

MEDICAL PROBLEMS RESULTING FROM SEX

Sex imposes a very considerable strain on the body and it is inevitable that from time to time this strain takes its toll. Many medical disorders seen by GPs or casualty departments arise directly or indirectly as a result of sexual activity. Some of the more common medical by-products of sex are as follows:

Housemaid's knee This is the build-up of fluid on the knee which normally results from too much kneeling. This is a common result of some of the more adventurous sexual positions, and of having sex with housemaids.

In-growing toe nails Positions which require balancing on the toes can put pressure on the soft tissue surrounding the toenails, causing them to grow inwards.

In-growing gonads The result, in most instances, of just too much sex.

In-growing sweat glands A common by-product of too much sex in warm climates.

Headaches Sex results in an increase in blood pressure, and this often leads to headaches. Headaches may also arise when the going gets really good but the bed is too close to the wall, resulting in head impact. Headaches may also be the result of worrying (for example about whether anyone is watching, whether you will actually be able to do it this time, whether she has taken the Pill, or whether that vasectomy scar is real etc).

Venereal disease Technically any disease directly transmitted through sexual activity. There are several to choose from.

Brainache Either the result of over-exertion, or the result of trying hard, and unsuccessfully, to think of a new position under stress (like he/she threatens to go home if it's the same as last time).

Stomach ache A common problem resulting from jumping into bed too soon after the romantic dinner.

Muscle sprains One of the commonest medical problems caused by sex. Sprained arms and legs are particularly common, though sprained tongues, toes, fingers, ear-lobes, vocal cords, etc. are not rare. Occasionally total sprain of the endocrine or lymphatic system is seen, and can be fatal.

Hernias Common in men as a result of too much effort.

Broken jaws Also common in men as a result of too little effort.

Fallen arches Normally the result of too much sex standing up, when the constant up and down movement weakens the bones of the foot causing the arch to fall.

Fallen kneecaps The inevitable result of fallen arches which spread upwards.

Fallen crutch An even more serious condition.

Impact injuries The most serious affecting the male sex organ itself, when a determined strike misses the target completely and attempts to penetrate the bed, pillow, floor or wall instead. Can be exceptionally painful.

Torsion of the testes Again the result of really strenuous going. One of the most painful conditions known to man.

Total deafness One of the hazards of aural sex (i.e.,sex involving the ears in any way).

Baldness It is not uncommon for female partners, at the moment of orgasm, to take an almighty tug at their partner's hair.

Loosened teeth Often a by-product of oral sex.

Loosened tonsils A by-product of more frisky oral sex.

Loosened vocal cords. Either the ultimate risk of oral sex, or the result of really strenuous moaning.

AIDS Exclusively a Gay Sex complaint, as are jolly sore buttocks, outrageously whipped thighs, jaunty rashes, light-hearted sprains, and reckless heart failure.

Eye strain Common in poorly lit bedrooms where finding your partner can be challenging.

Allergies Common allergies are to rubber, vinyl, armadillo skin, leather, suede, PVC, Vaseline, engine oil, battery acid (often the result of using an old-fashioned vibrator incorporating rechargeable accumulators), glass bottles, various items of cheap cutlery.

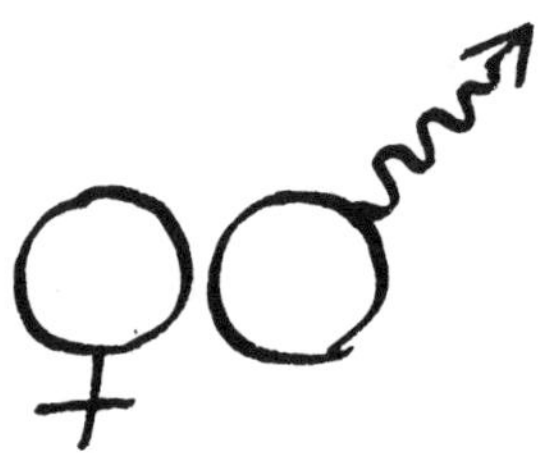

'I told you it was dangerous.'

PSYCHOLOGICAL PROBLEMS RESULTING FROM SEX

In addition to the catalogue of medical problems which result directly from sex, there is the ever-present risk of psychological damage. Some of the more common problems are:

Identity crises When you discover the next morning that your partner was the wrong sex, but you find you don't seem to mind.

Lack of self-esteem When you find you hate yourself in the morning.

Self-hate A more extreme form of lack of self-esteem, as when for example you discover the next morning that it was the entire Cardiff Rugby Team.

Split personality When you really enjoyed it but still hate yourself the next day.

Guilt A very common result of sex, often caused by outnumbering your partner's orgasms 10 to 1, wanting to make love all the time except when voting for your Euro-MP, having sex with your Euro-MP when he/she should be in Brussels, having sex with someone you don't really love, masturbation, having lustful feelings towards Porsche 928s or agricultural tractors, enjoying sex knowing more than half the world doesn't have enough to eat or enough electro-vibrators, etc, etc.

'Your husband's worried about you . . .'

Loss of memory Very common in the males of the species, who often forget they are married.

Paranoia Usually worry that your mother-in-law can hear or see what is going on.

Persecution When your patner always insists on choosing which position, or which side of the bed to lie on, or what whip to use, or whether it will be rubber, suede or vinyl tonight, etc.

Withdrawal A common condition in the male arising when his partner says at the crucial moment that she has not taken any precautions.

'What's a transvestite, Mum?'

SEX AND THE LAW

The law places some fairly rigid controls over our sexual lives. The most important legal aspects are as follows:

- your partner must be willing.
- your partner must be over the age of consent.
- your partner must not be more closely related to you than cousin.
- you must not make love in such a way as to threaten the stability of the ruling government.
- you must not make love in such a way as to obstruct the Queen's highway. (For this reason alone, the M1's hard shoulder is not recommended regardless of lead levels.)
- you must make love within the spirit of, if not the letter of, the Geneva Convention.
- you must not make love merely to avoid paying tax.
- if you earn more than £15,000 a year from sex you must register for VAT.
- you must not make love inside naval dockyards wearing low flashpoint clothing. (Remember arson in such locations is still a capital offence.)
- sex must not impinge on the flight-paths near any major airport. (In practice this means keeping clear of airspace above 2000 feet.)
- you must not make love on a cross-Channel ferry with more than one litre of spirit on your person.
- you must not chase your partner at more than 70 mph except on private land.
- you must not make love to more than one of your wives at any one time.
- your partner must be of the same species as yourself.
- you must not make love in such a way as to make any onlookers die laughing; this could expose you to a charge of manslaughter.
- you must not have sex in either of the chambers of Parliament whilst Parliament is sitting. (Normally they will want to stand in any case to get a better view.)
- you must not make love in such a way as to call into question the laws of gravity. (Although not technically a criminal action, the possible consequences are just as grave.)
- if sex substantially alters the use of your premises you must seek planning consent, and remain at all times within the requirements of the Building Regulations. (Any erection of any sort must satisfy these regulations.)

1000 NEW EXCUSES

EXCUSES FOR MORE OR LESS SEX

The real reason why you may wish to have more, or have less, sex with a particular partner is that you fancy them a lot, or don't fancy them at all. However, such reasons are rather on the blunt side for most people to accept, particularly if you wish to preserve some degree of romance in the relationship. It is therefore a good idea to couch your desire for a higher or lower frequency of sexual activity in a more intellectual way; this not only gets the message across, but may also impress your partner to some degree. Below we suggest a number of ways of bidding for more or less sex:

Excuses for More Sex

- sex helps extend the metaphysical psyche into potentially quasi-latent dimensions.
- sex assists the patent psycho-physiological manifestation of the culturally oriented yin/yang conflict inherent in the human condition's underlying subconscious.
- sex helps resolve the fundamental retrogressive auto-suppressive internalized hetero-homo sexual preference conflict embedded in the father/mother image type interface.
- sex stops you going blind.

Excuses for Less Sex

- sex hinders the extension of the metaphysical psyche into potentially quasi-latent dimensions.
- sex prevents the patent psycho physiological manifestation of the culturally oriented yin/yang conflict inherent in the human condition's underlying subconscious.
- sex hinders the resolution of the fundamental retrogressive auto-suppressive internalized hetero-homo sexual preference conflict embedded in the father/mother image type interface.
- sex makes you go blind.

(These excuses are OK so long as your partner is not a psychiatrist. If your partner is a psychiatrist it is best to stick to the old 'I've got a headache' if you want less sex, and 'Isn't it time we did it again?' if you want more sex.)

SEX UNDER ADVERSE CONDITIONS

Many people find that after many years of active sex even the most unusual variation or position fails to give the extra stimulus required for really exciting and satisfying love-making. At the same time many such people will have observed that whenever sex has actually been achieved under adverse conditions, and against all odds, the result has been unusually rewarding. This suggests that it might be well worth while people going out of their way to create such adverse conditions in order to inject excitement and challenge back into a waning sex life. Some of the adverse conditions which have been brought to the author's attention are as follows:

- during a job interview (particularly if you subsequently got the job in spite of your partner not being the interviewer).
- whilst being baptized/confirmed or whilst receiving communion.
- during the wedding ceremony, especially if your partner is the vicar or his wife.
- underwater. The satisfaction depends to a large extent on how long you can hold your breath.
- during a free-fall parachute jump.
- while taking the driving test. Especially challenging if you manage to continue throughout the emergency stop and still pass.
- during a dental extraction.
- while driving down the M1 the wrong way in the fast lane.
- while discussing your mortgage application with the local manager of your building society.
- while your mother-in-law is watching.
- while your mother-in-law is scoring.
- during an appeal against an income tax assessment.
- while the jury is returning its verdict during your trial for indecent exposure.
- while tuning a piano, especially if it is in the Albert Hall.
- while competing in the Olympic bobsleigh event.
- while a Barry Manilow record is playing in the background.
- while having a vasectomy.

SEX AND PERSONAL HYGIENE

Sex is a particularly intimate experience (nearly as intimate as having a joint bank account) and a certain degree of personal hygiene is thought of by most people as essential (in other words if you smell like a pig most people will refuse to go to bed with you). The basic requirements are that you are clean and fresh, well presented in clean clothes, and have a clean bed available. In most instances these basic requirements are not difficult to meet (at the North Pole in a force 12 Arctic blizzard it is not so easy, but there again neither is sex under such conditions, even if you can find a partner). Particular personal hygiene pitfalls to avoid are:

- wax oozing out of your ears.
- wax oozing out of your navel.
- wax oozing out of any other bodily orifice, especially if it is an unusual colour, or moves of its own accord.
- secretions dripping from your nose. (Hint: always blow your nose well beforehand, even if you haven't got a cold. By the time you are in bed it could be too late.)
- skid marks on your pants or knickers.
- juice stains on your shorts.
- large spot or blackhead on the tip of your nose. This can become an amazing distraction when things get really intimate.
- dirty fingernails. Also make sure your nails are not too long otherwise severe lacerations may result.

'No clean socks, buttons falling off, no cooked breakfast . . . Lord knows why I married you.'

'That was your second bath this month . . . Have you got a fancy woman?'

- dirty toe nails. Again beware long sharp nails, as these can devastate the bed clothes if things get lively.
- long, dirty hair. If your partner has to concentrate on avoiding swipes from your long, greasy, nit-ridden locks it is certain that he/she will not concentrate on you.
- bad breath. If your partner winces every time you whisper some sweet nothing in his/her ear, then you can be sure the nothings are sweeter than your breath.
- stubble on the chin. Ensure a stubble-free chin in order to avoid multiple punctures on your partner. Women in particular should pay special attention to this point.
- sweaty armpits. The armpits can become fairly ripe after one or two hours of sex, and it is wise to invest in a powerful underarm deodorant.
- sweaty crutch. Again some personal hygiene preparation for the crutch is a good idea, but avoid hair cream on the pubic hair.

SEX AND THE WEATHER

Sex is one activity for which the weather is always ideal. For example:

When it is raining . . . you might as well stay indoors and keep dry, and if you are stuck indoors what better thing to do than go to bed and make love?

When it is cold . . . what better way to warm up?

When it is hot . . . people generally start taking off their clothes, and once the clothes start to come off then thoughts turn lightly to the idea of making love.

When the sun shines . . . everyone feels happier and friendlier, and when people get friendly what happens? Anyway, if you went out you might get sun stroke.

When there is the risk of a hurricane . . . it is wise to cling on to some object for safety, and what better object to choose than someone of the opposite sex.

When it is foggy . . . it is best to remain in familiar surroundings otherwise you might get lost, and what better familiar surroundings to remain in than your own bed. And it seems silly to stay there all day alone.

When it is snowing . . . what better way to appreciate the beauty of snow than to watch it from a bedroom window?

During a thunderstorm . . . many people need comfort and security. So do the decent thing and find yourself one of these people and offer comfort and security, and what better place to do this than in the comfort and security of bed?

During a drought . . . it is vital not to move around too much and lose precious body fluid. Therefore why move further than your own bed. And in order not to get too lonely invite a friend to join you.

Indeed, the author has investigated virtually all historically recorded climatic conditions, and without exception they all appear ideal for sexual activity. The author has undertaken, purely from an unselfish scientific motivation, to monitor on a day-to-day basis the suitability of the British climate for sexual activity, and expects to be able to make an authoritative statement in around 15 years' time.

*'I think Mr Grimshaw fancies you, Mabel.
That's the second time this week he's put his teeth in.'*

SEX AND AGE

There is no fundamental reason why sexual activity should decrease in either sex because of advancing years. Indeed there are certain advantages that the old enjoy which the young don't, like less risk of pregnancy, more free time for sex, and less risk of disturbance from young children. As long as you take things fairly easy, and choose your partner with care, there is no reason at all why you shouldn't bask in an active sex life way into your nineties. The only things you should take care about are the following:

- the risk of your teeth falling out and denting your partner. Rattling teeth can also be something of a passion-killer.
- dribbling and slobbering over your partner due to reduced control of the facial muscles.
- hearing-aid interference, and positive feedback deafening both yourself and your partner. Make sure your hearing aid doesn't fall out; it ruins the mood if you respond to things like 'more, more, oh please, more . . . just like that . . .' with statements like 'I can't hear a bloody word . . . hearing aid must be on the blink again.'
- zimmer frame and walking-stick-inflicted injuries.
- extra wear and tear on artificial hips.
- the need for bifocals to identify different erogenous zones.
- difficulty in telling whether your partner is actually undressed or still wearing creased flesh-coloured clothes.
- poor memory, causing you to forget what you got into bed for. And tiredness which makes you fall asleep before you remember.
- difficulty in climbing into bed without help from district nurse.
- difficulty in climbing on to partner without help from district nurse.
- impotence on pension day due to excitement of seeing money again.
- chin or chins dragging on bed or floor.
- worry about pension keeping pace with inflation.
- bone-creak.
- knees getting locked.

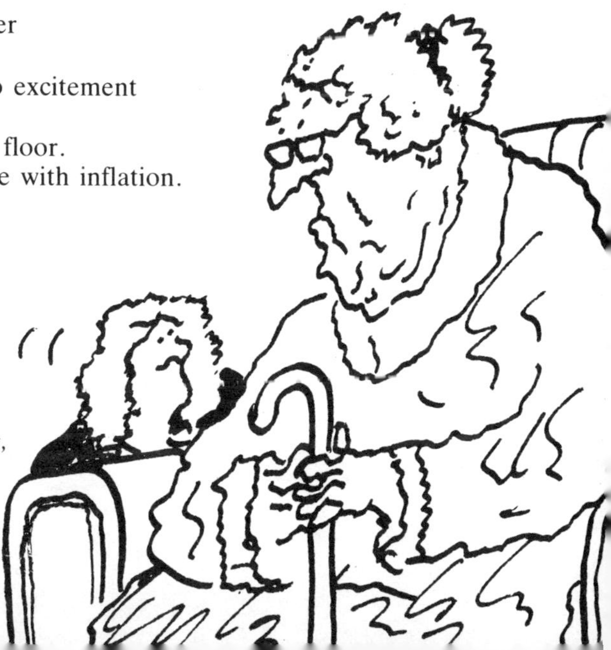

'Had sex been invented when you were young, Grandma?'

SEX AND POLITICS

It is interesting to compare and contrast sex and politics. They have quite a lot in common, including:

- both can often get boring.
- both are open to men and women.
- a lot of both go on in the Westminster area of London.
- both politicians and lovers say a lot of meaningless things.
- both often don't tell the whole truth, and are constantly worried about being found out.
- no formal qualifications are required for either.
- there is a minimum age for legal participation in both.
- both are often associated with parties.
- both sometimes involve whips.
- both sometimes result in Bills, although sex can result in Freds, Sarahs, and Johns as well.
- one is full of elections and the other full of erections.
- both often take place late into the night.
- both are sometimes done mainly for money.
- in both cases some people think of England when they do it.
- in both it is easy to fall out of favour quickly.

In terms of differences it is interesting to note that sex is usually:

- quicker.
- generally more pleasurable but carries a higher risk of disease.
- generally done in the company of fewer people and hence can be cosier.
- not the subject of four-yearly reselection.
- in most cases does not take a summer recess.
- not salaried.

'If your wife doesn't understand you, Mr Wilkins, you ought to try speaking a bit more clearly to her.'

'Cut the crap, Dad . . . just tell me did Snow White have a dwarf fetish or not?'

FAMOUS SAYINGS ABOUT SEX

Over the years many important statements and observations about sex have been made by the famous both in real life and in literature. However, in earlier, more prudish ages many of these statements became veiled in innuendo or euphemism; it is only now, in our more enlightened age, that many of these statements can be read in their original form. Below we reproduce in unexpurgated form some of the more important of these statements:*

'Is this a ****** that I see before me? Come, let me hold it.'

'A ****, a *****, my kingdom for a ****!'

'Never before in the field of human ********* have so many owed so much to so few.'

'Hell hath no fury like a woman *****ed.'

'To ***, or not to ***, that is the question.'

'****** me, Hardy.'

'Off with his *****'

'Reports of my ***** are greatly exaggerated.'

'I bring you ****** in our time.'

'You've never had it so good.'

'I may have the **** of a frail and feeble woman, but I have the **** of a man.'

*Unfortunately due to last-minute advice from counsel it was deemed necessary to censor most of these quotations.

THE
GUIDE TO
SEX